STATE V. DELANEY

Third Edition

State v. Delaney

Third Edition

Joseph E. Taylor

Professor Emeritus of Law
McGeorge School of Law
University of the Pacific
Sacramento, California

and

A. J. Griffith-Reed

Administration & Technology Specialist
Institute for Administrative Justice
McGeorge School of Law
University of the Pacific

Address inquiries to:
Reprint Permission
National Institute for Trial Advocacy
1685 38th Street, Suite 200
Boulder, CO 80301-2735
Phone: (800) 225-6482
Fax: (720) 890-7069
Email: permissions@nita.org

ISBN 978-1-60156-715-4
eISBN 978-1-60156-716-1
FBA 1715

Printed in the United States of America

CONTENTS

ACKNOWLEDGMENTS

The authors would like to acknowledge the special contribution to the development of this case made by Dr. Elizabeth Loftus, a Distinguished Professor in the Department of Psychology and Social Behavior, the Department of Criminology, Law, and Society, and the Department of Cognitive Sciences, and a Fellow of The Center for the Neurobiology of Learning and Memory at the University of California, Irvine, and a Professor of Psychology at the University of Washington. She is a nationally recognized expert in eyewitness identification. Dr. Loftus supplied specialized information that was especially helpful in preparing the defense expert report and greatly assisted the authors in formulating the case. Counsel for the prosecution and for the defense in this case would benefit greatly in their preparation for trial by reading the book *Eyewitness Testimony: Civil and Criminal*, Third Edition by Dr. Loftus and James M. Doyle. That work discusses, in considerable detail, the dynamics of the human memory and offers suggestions for direct and cross-examination of eyewitnesses and experts.

The graphics, including the diagram and maps, the news article, and the fingerprint comparison display were all prepared by Lori Hall, head of the Graphics Department of McGeorge School of Law.

Special thanks to Facebook and Vecteezy.com for use of images from their sites.

Thanks also to Jeffrey Smith, Supervising Identification Technician for the Sacramento Police Department, for the expert fingerprint identification information used in the case and for providing the fingerprint exhibits.

Our appreciation to Nick Guzzetta of Guzzetta Jewelers of Sacramento for his help in providing scene photos in the case and advice about the jewelry business.

And, Joseph Taylor's special thanks to Vincent Reagor of Nine Mile Falls, Washington, who was his supervisor and mentor during his years as a prosecuting attorney, and who assisted him greatly in preparing and trying the original Delaney case. Vince Reagor had a greater impact on the training of Deputy D.A. Joseph Taylor than any other teacher or attorney. He taught him how to prepare cases for trial, how to present the case in court, and perhaps most importantly, what ethical responsibilities prosecuting attorneys bear and how to fulfill those responsibilities. Joseph Taylor worked with many prosecuting attorneys for over twenty-two years, and he placed Vince Reagor at the top of that cast. Vince passed away last year, and Joseph Taylor will truly miss this remarkable man.

Lastly, we would like to acknowledge the 1947 Chicago Cubs. Although they did not win the National League pennant that year, they did leave a fond and lasting impression, evidenced by the fact that all thirty-one members of that team are mentioned in the case.

INTRODUCTION

This is a criminal case in which Ardell Delaney has been charged with a violation of Section 211 of the Criminal Code of the State of Nita, the felony of armed robbery.

The defendant, Ardell Delaney, a professional baseball player, was a top pitcher for the University of Nita baseball team. He was drafted by the Nita City Nighthawks and played for three different Nighthawks farm teams. In the late spring of YR-1, he injured his throwing arm and was on the disabled list throughout the summer of YR-1.

He has been accused of robbing at gunpoint Lexi Waitkus, the assistant manager of Miller's Fine Jewelers, in the early evening of September 14, YR-1. The armed robber escaped with approximately $22,440. On September 21, YR-1, the Nita Police Department arrested Val Cavarretta for possession for sale of cocaine. Detective Alex Lowrey interviewed Cavarretta about the offense, and Cavarretta told Detective Lowrey that Cavarretta planned to sell cocaine to Ardell Delaney. Cavarretta claimed Delaney had money from a recent robbery of a jewelry store. Detective Lowrey checked with the Nita City Police Department (NCPD) Identification Section and found that a print from a silver dollar taken from the robbery and found nearby bore seven points of similarity with Delaney's print. Lowrey then obtained a court order to take Delaney into limited custody for a lineup. On September 22, YR-1, Lowrey conducted a lineup in which Waitkus identified the defendant. Delaney was arrested. The District Court for the County of Darrow held a preliminary hearing on October 20, YR-1. The defendant pleaded not guilty to the charge, and the case is now set for trial.

The defendant contends that this is a case of mistaken identification, and he claims that at the time of the robbery he was having his car checked for emissions certification. He also claims that the Nita City Police Department conducted a grossly unfair lineup identification procedure.

The applicable law is contained in the proposed jury instructions set forth at the end of the file.

All years in these materials are stated in the following form:

- YR-0 indicates the actual year in which the case is being tried (i.e., the present year);
- YR-1 indicates the next preceding year (please use the actual year);
- YR-2 indicates the second preceding year (please use the actual year), etc.

Electronic, color copies of all exhibits can be found at the following website:

http://bit.ly/1P20Jea
Password: Delaney3

Special Instructions for Use as a Full Trial

When this case file is used for a full trial, each party is limited to calling the following witnesses:

State of Nita:

- Lexi Waitkus
- Detective Alex Lowrey
- Val Cavarretta
- Supervising ID Technician Jan Nicholson

Defendant:

- Ardell Delaney
- Dr. Leslie Scheffing
- Marty Pafko
- Pepper Hack

Discovery Obligations

Nita Criminal Code Section 1054.3 requires the defense to disclose names, addresses, relevant written statements, and reports of witnesses that the defense intends to call at trial. Pursuant to that code section, the reports of defense witnesses Pepper Hack, Marty Pafko, and Dr. Scheffing have been disclosed to the prosecution.

Pursuant to Nita Criminal Code Section 1054.2, Nita City Police Department case reports were disclosed to the defense by the prosecution, except the report relating to Val Cavarretta. The court in a specially conducted hearing then required the prosecution to also release the Cavarretta report to the defense, which the prosecution did.

Required Stipulations

1) The defendant Ardell Delaney is male. All other witnesses may be either male or female.

2) The lineup conducted on September 24, YR-1, consisted of six male subjects all of the same race as the defendant and the same age group as the defendant. The weights of each did not vary by more than ten pounds, and the heights did not vary by more than two inches. None of the subjects, including the defendant, had any unusual identifying marks on their faces.

3) The inked official print card fingerprint impression referred to by Jan Nicholson as the defendant's at pages 7, 17 and 55 was, in fact, the left index fingerprint of Ardell Delaney made on April 10, YR-7. Counsel may not contest the identification of the print, but may contest whether the date of the print is admissible.

4) Lexi Waitkus, in initially describing the robber, identified the robber's race to be the same as the subject playing the role of the defendant (see pages 47 and 85).

PRETRIAL MOTIONS

The defendant moved to suppress the statement he made to Detective Lowrey on Fifth, Sixth, and Fourteenth Amendment grounds, citing *Miranda v. Arizona*, 384 U.S. 436, 444 (1966). The court denied the motion. The defendant also moved to suppress evidence of the previous eyewitness identification by Lexi Waitkus, as well as any present in-court identification by Waitkus as the product of a constitutionally impermissible and unduly suggestive identification. The court denied that motion. These legal issues may not be relitigated at trial, although the defendant is entitled to litigate the unreliability of the identification to the jury.

Additionally, the defense moved to exclude any testimony or exhibits referring in any way to social media, Facebook, or text messages that the prosecution would offer as evidence in this case. The court declined to rule on those issues until the court hears more specific information from both counsel.

IN THE DISTRICT COURT OF
THE STATE OF NITA
COUNTY OF DARROW

THE STATE OF NITA	)	
	)	Case No. CR 1909-YR-1
vs.	)	
	)	INFORMATION
ARDELL PATRICK DELANEY,	)	
Defendant.	)	
	)	

THE STATE OF NITA does hereby charge the defendant, ARDELL PATRICK DELANEY, with the following offense under the Criminal Code of the State of Nita:

That on the 14th day of September, YR-1, at and within the County of Darrow and within the boundaries of Nita City, Ardell Patrick Delaney did commit the crime of Robbery of the First Degree, a felony, in violation of Section 211 of the Criminal Code of the State of Nita, in that he did knowingly, willfully, feloniously, and unlawfully take by force or fear from the person or immediate presence of Lexi Waitkus the sum of approximately **$22,440** in lawful U.S. currency with the intent to permanently deprive Lexi Waitkus and Miller's Fine Jewelers of this money, and that at that time Ardell Patrick Delaney was armed with and did use a handgun, to wit, a revolver.

DATED: November 3, YR-1

Melissa Anne Fox
Melissa Anne Fox, District Attorney
Darrow County
State of Nita

EXHIBITS

Electronic, color copies of all exhibits can be found at the following website:

http://bit.ly/1P20Jea
Password: Delaney3

Exhibit 1

INTERIOR OF MILLER'S FINE JEWELERS

Exhibit 2

Safe

Exhibit 3

Area of Recovery of Bag and Silver Dollar

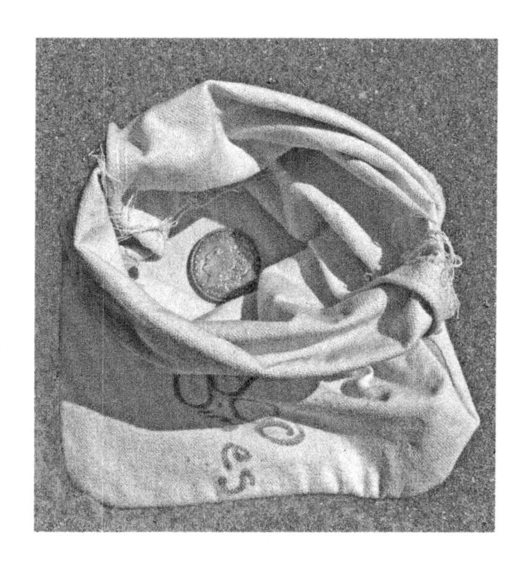

Exhibit 4

Latent Fingerprint from Silver Dollar

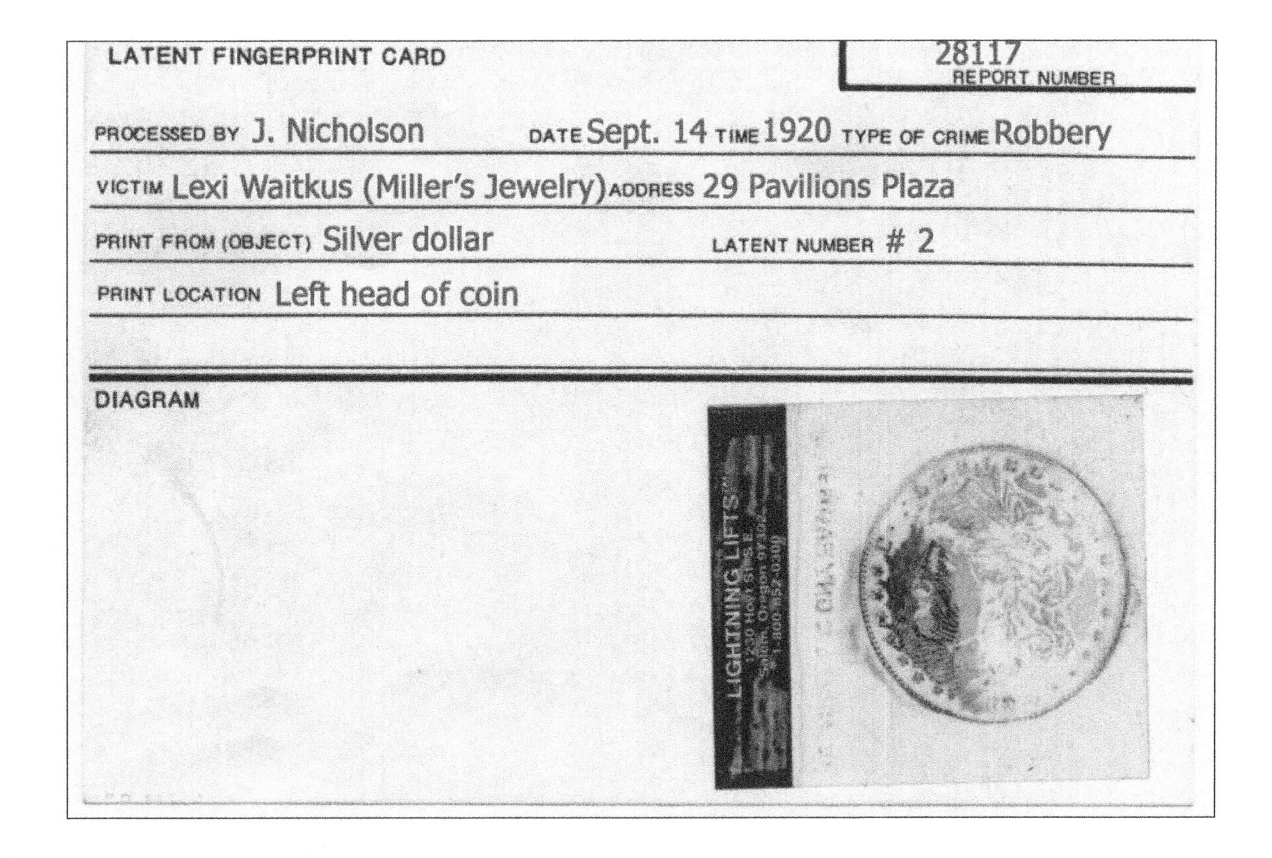

LATENT FINGERPRINT CARD

28117
REPORT NUMBER

PROCESSED BY J. Nicholson DATE Sept. 14 TIME 1920 TYPE OF CRIME Robbery

VICTIM Lexi Waitkus (Miller's Jewelry) ADDRESS 29 Pavilions Plaza

PRINT FROM (OBJECT) Silver dollar LATENT NUMBER # 2

PRINT LOCATION Left head of coin

DIAGRAM

Exhibit 5

COMPARISON OF LATENT PRINT WITH DELANEY'S PRINT

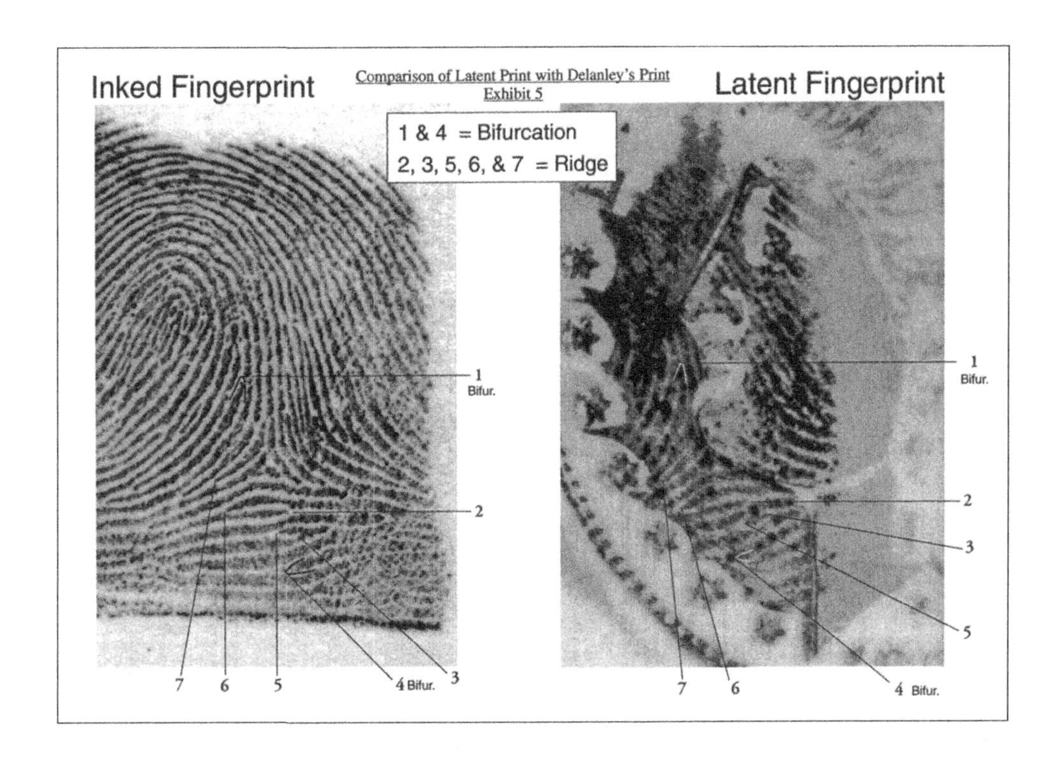

Exhibit 6

Ardell Delaney's Baseball Cap

Exhibit 7

Diagram of Miller's Fine Jewelers

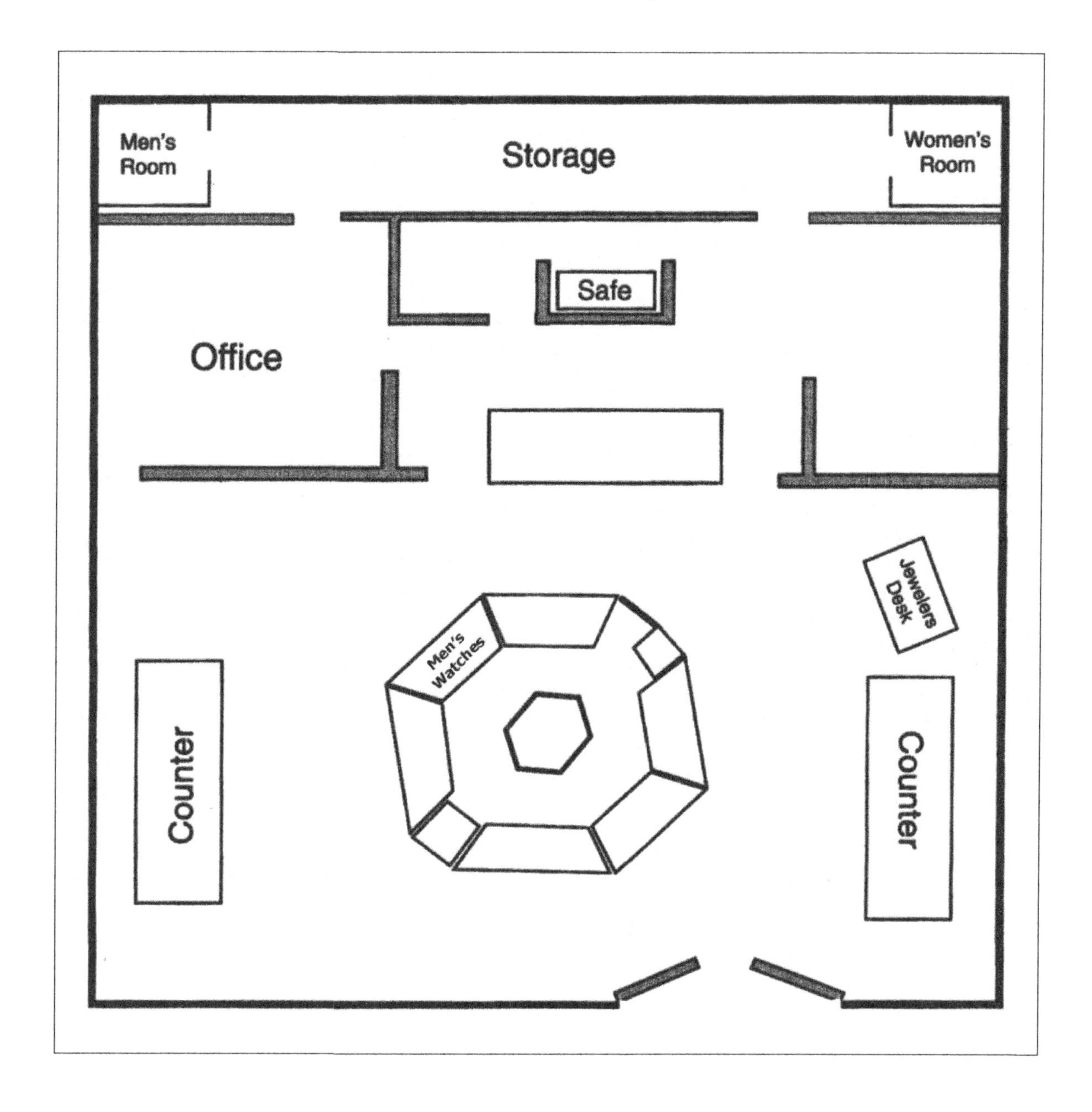

Exhibit 8

Map of Pavilions Plaza

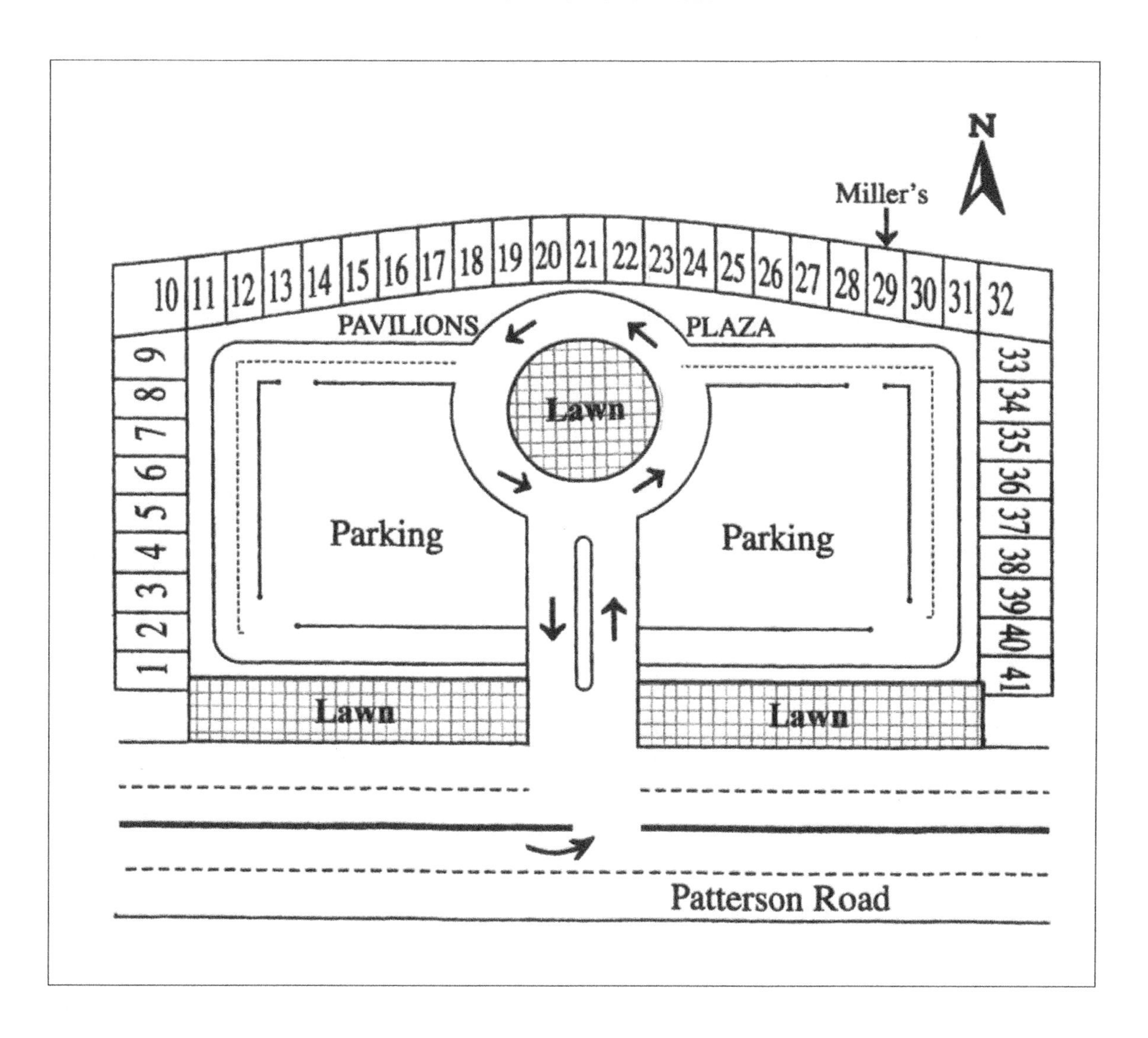

Exhibit 9

Map of Nita City

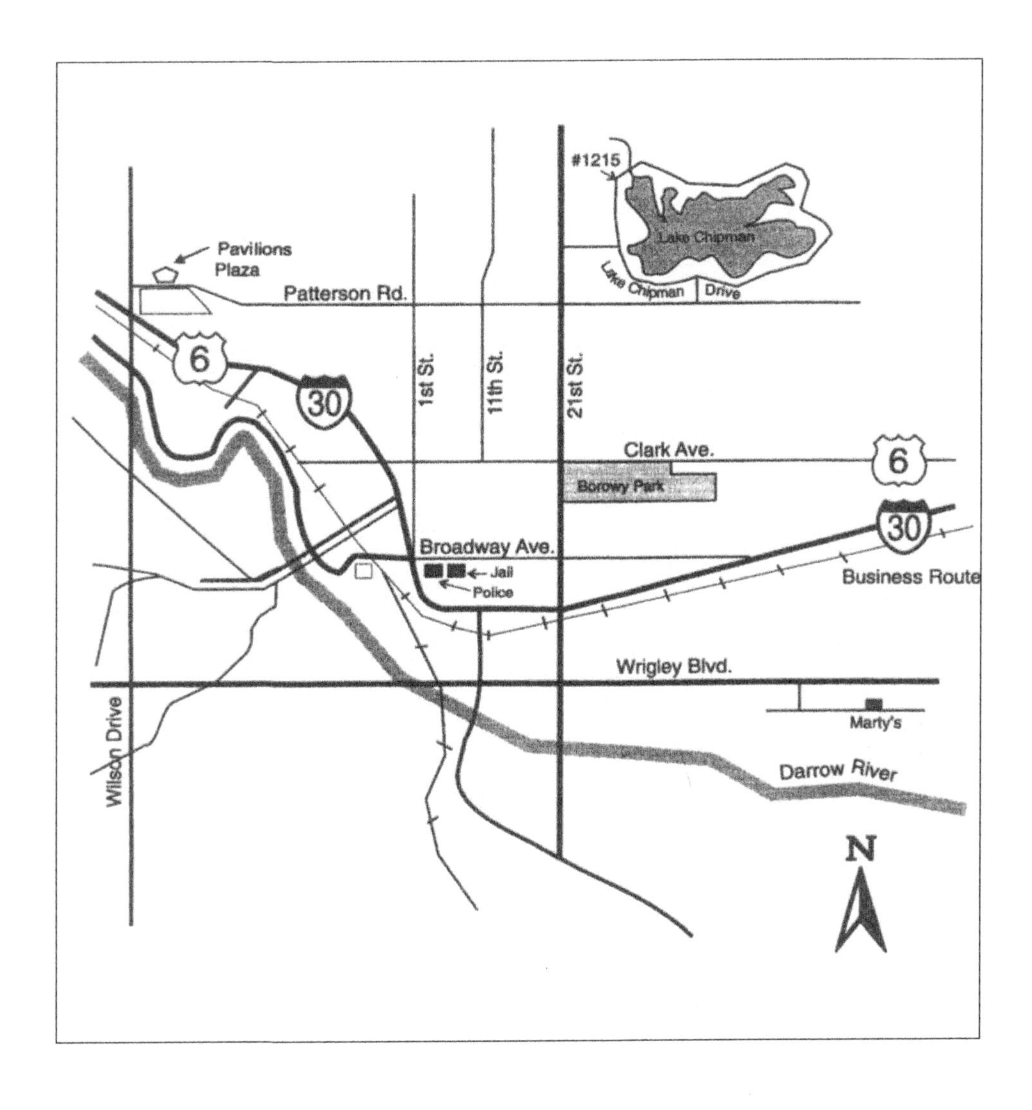

Exhibit 10

Search for people, places and things
The Nasties Home Find Friends
the nasties
JUL
21
The Nasties
Public • Concert • Hosted by The Grove
✓ Interested
Invite
Edit
July 21, YR-1 at 9pm
The Grove, Nita City
EVENT TIPS
Next Tip
Events Tips Website
Learn how to get more people to your events by following the tips on the event website.
See Website
About
Discussion
Write Post
Add Photo/Video
Create Poll
Write Something......
108
Interested
273
Went
1K
Invited
Details
The Nasties
Pre-sale: $20 http://bit.ly/nastiesgrove39ls

Exhibit 11

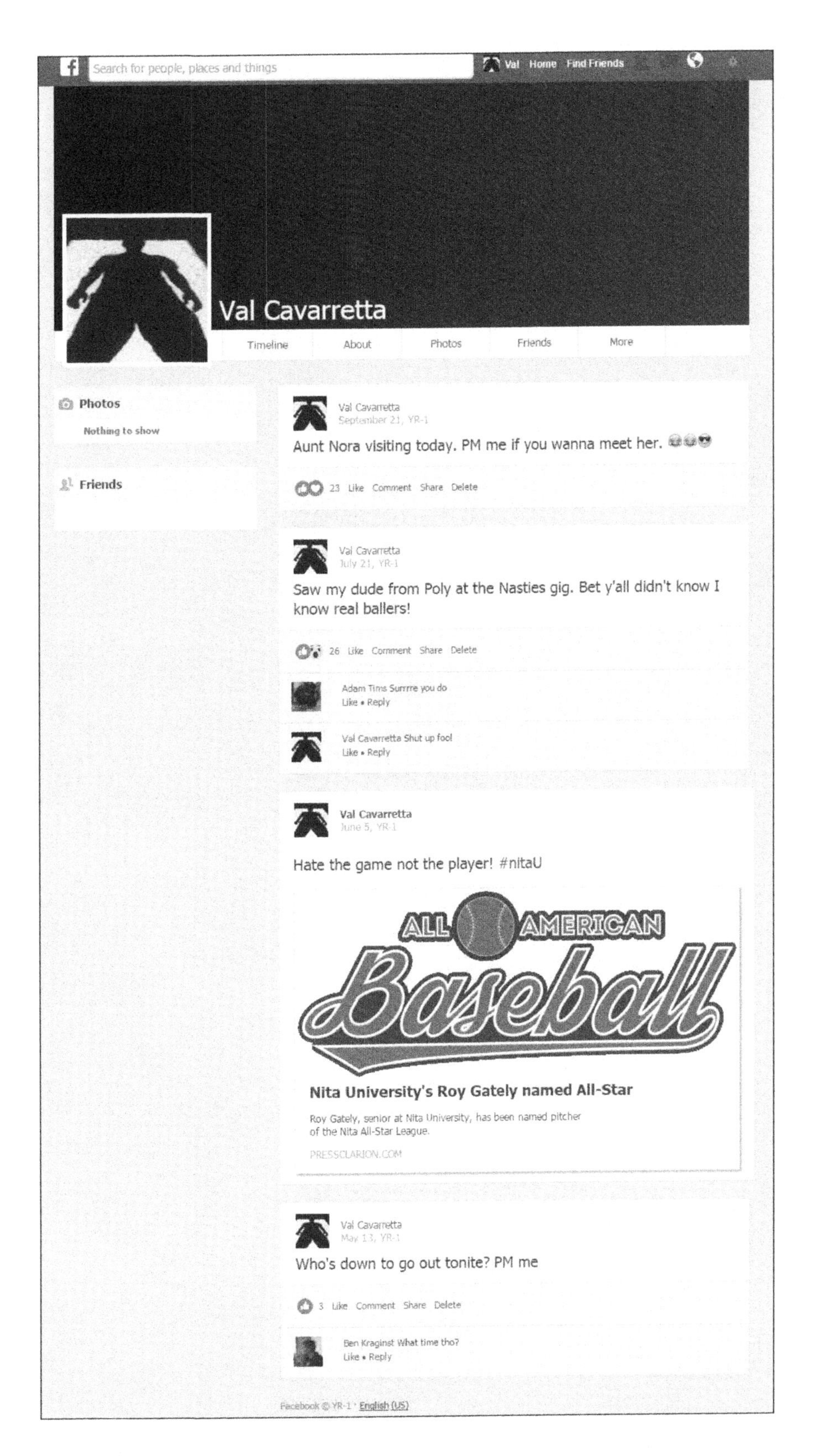
Search for people, places and things
Val Home Find Friends
Val Cavarretta
Timeline About Photos Friends More
Photos
Nothing to show
Friends
Val Cavarretta
September 21, YR-1
Aunt Nora visiting today. PM me if you wanna meet her.
23 Like Comment Share Delete
Val Cavarretta
July 21, YR-1
Saw my dude from Poly at the Nasties gig. Bet y'all didn't know I know real ballers!
26 Like Comment Share Delete
Adam Tims Surrrre you do
Like • Reply
Val Cavarretta Shut up fool
Like • Reply
Val Cavarretta
June 5, YR-1
Hate the game not the player! #nitaU
ALL AMERICAN
Baseball
Nita University's Roy Gately named All-Star
Roy Gately, senior at Nita University, has been named pitcher of the Nita All-Star League.
PRESSCLARION.COM
Val Cavarretta
May 13, YR-1
Who's down to go out tonite? PM me
3 Like Comment Share Delete
Ben Kraginst What time tho?
Like • Reply
Facebook © YR-1 · English (US)

Exhibit 12

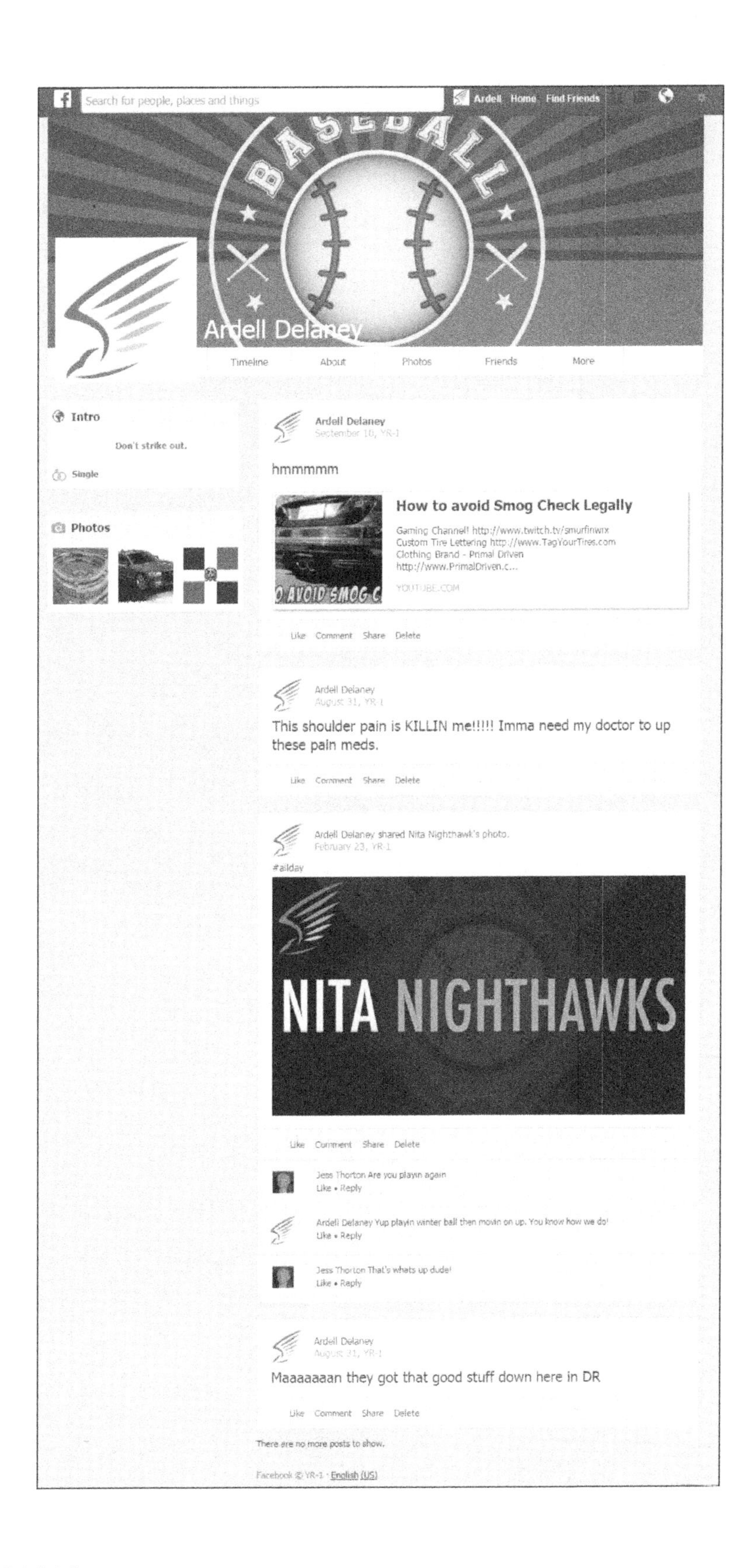
Search for people, places and things
Ardell Home Find Friends
BASEBALL
Ardell Delaney
Timeline
About
Photos
Friends
More
Intro
Don't strike out.
Single
Photos
Ardell Delaney
September 10, YR-1
hmmmmm
How to avoid Smog Check Legally
Gaming Channel! http://www.twitch.tv/smurfinwrx
Custom Tire Lettering http://www.TagYourTires.com
Clothing Brand - Primal Driven
http://www.PrimalDriven.c...
YOUTUBE.COM
O AVOID SMOG C
Like Comment Share Delete
Ardell Delaney
August 31, YR-1
This shoulder pain is KILLIN me!!!!! Imma need my doctor to up these pain meds.
Like Comment Share Delete
Ardell Delaney shared Nita Nighthawk's photo.
February 23, YR-1
#allday
NITA NIGHTHAWKS
Like Comment Share Delete
Jess Thorton Are you playin again
Like • Reply
Ardell Delaney Yup playin winter ball then movin on up. You know how we do!
Like • Reply
Jess Thorton That's whats up dude!
Like • Reply
Ardell Delaney
August 31, YR-1
Maaaaaaan they got that good stuff down here in DR
Like Comment Share Delete
There are no more posts to show.
Facebook © YR-1 · English (US)

Exhibit 13

Marty's Repairs
Marty's Repairs
Home
Find Friends
MARTY'S AUTO REPAIRS
3914 DALLESANDRO WAY, NITA CITY
MARTY'S AUTO REPAIRS
Marty's Repairs
@martysrepairs
Home
Posts
Photos
About
Likes
Create a page
Liked
Following
Share
··· More
Call Now
Satus
Photo/Video
Write something......
Marty's Repairs
September 1, YR-1
We partner with Smog 'N Stop to take care of your smog inspection needs. Book the bundle service when you bring your car in, and we'll take it over to be smogged for you once we're finished with your repairs.
1 Like Comment Share
Marilyn Kemps Wait, you guys don't do smog checks?
Like • Reply
Marty's Repairs No, but if you get a repair at our shop you'll get a discount when you go to Smog 'N Stop.
Like • Reply
Marilyn Kemps How much are their smog checks?
Like • Reply
Marty's Repairs Sorry ma'am, you'd need to contact them directly about your vehicle to find out exact pricing. We just give a 10% discount.
Like • Reply
Marty's Repairs
August 1, YR-1
Be sure to sign up for our email listing to get coupons and discounts!
Like Comment Share
Automotive
Search for posts on this Page
Invite friends to like this Page
We repair cars, trucks, and motorcycles at a reasonable cost.
77 Likes
Ardell Delaney likes this
About
(800) 288-6619
Message Now
Automotive
VISITOR POSTS
Marty Pakfo
February 13, YR-1
Looking for car parts? We've got you covered! Swing by and see if we have what you need.
Like • Comment

Exhibit 14

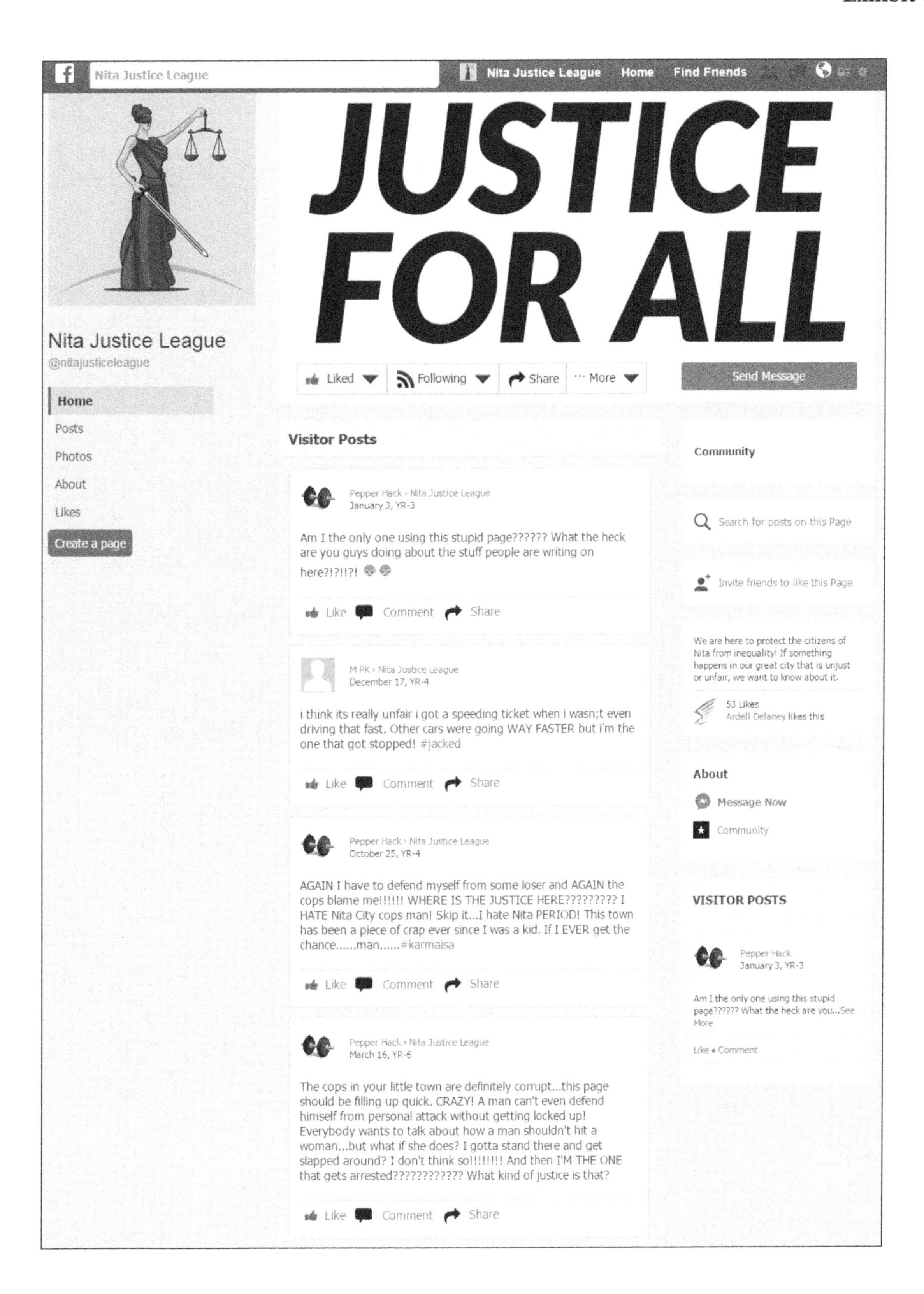

Nita Justice League
Nita Justice League
Home
Find Friends
JUSTICE FOR ALL
Nita Justice League
@nitajusticeleague
Home
Posts
Photos
About
Likes
Create a page
Liked
Following
Share
More
Send Message
Visitor Posts
Pepper Hack › Nita Justice League
January 3, YR-3
Am I the only one using this stupid page?????? What the heck are you guys doing about the stuff people are writing on here?!?!!?!
Like
Comment
Share
M PK › Nita Justice League
December 17, YR-4
i think its really unfair i got a speeding ticket when i wasn;t even driving that fast. Other cars were going WAY FASTER but i'm the one that got stopped! #jacked
Like
Comment
Share
Pepper Hack › Nita Justice League
October 25, YR-4
AGAIN I have to defend myself from some loser and AGAIN the cops blame me!!!!!! WHERE IS THE JUSTICE HERE????????? I HATE Nita City cops man! Skip it...I hate Nita PERIOD! This town has been a piece of crap ever since I was a kid. If I EVER get the chance......man......#karmaisa
Like
Comment
Share
Pepper Hack › Nita Justice League
March 16, YR-6
The cops in your little town are definitely corrupt...this page should be filling up quick. CRAZY! A man can't even defend himself from personal attack without getting locked up! Everybody wants to talk about how a man shouldn't hit a woman...but what if she does? I gotta stand there and get slapped around? I don't think so!!!!!!!! And then I'M THE ONE that gets arrested???????????? What kind of justice is that?
Like
Comment
Share
Community
Search for posts on this Page
Invite friends to like this Page
We are here to protect the citizens of Nita from inequality! If something happens in our great city that is unjust or unfair, we want to know about it.
53 Likes
Ardell Delaney likes this
About
Message Now
Community
VISITOR POSTS
Pepper Hack
January 3, YR-3
Am I the only one using this stupid page?????? What the heck are you...See More
Like • Comment

Exhibit 15

Texts from Val Cavarretta to Marty Pafko

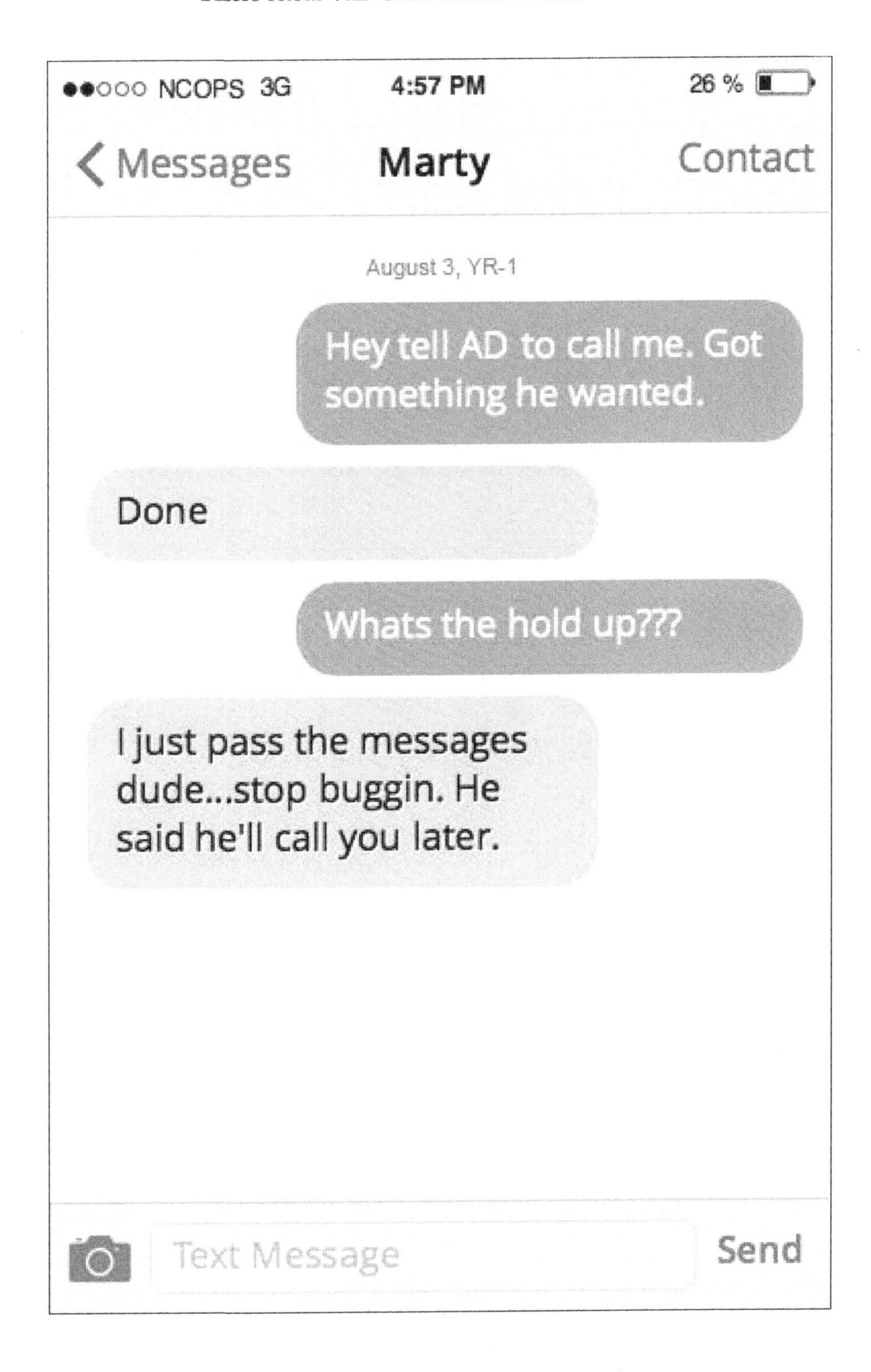

Exhibit 16

TEXTS FROM MARTY PAFKO TO ARDELL DELANEY

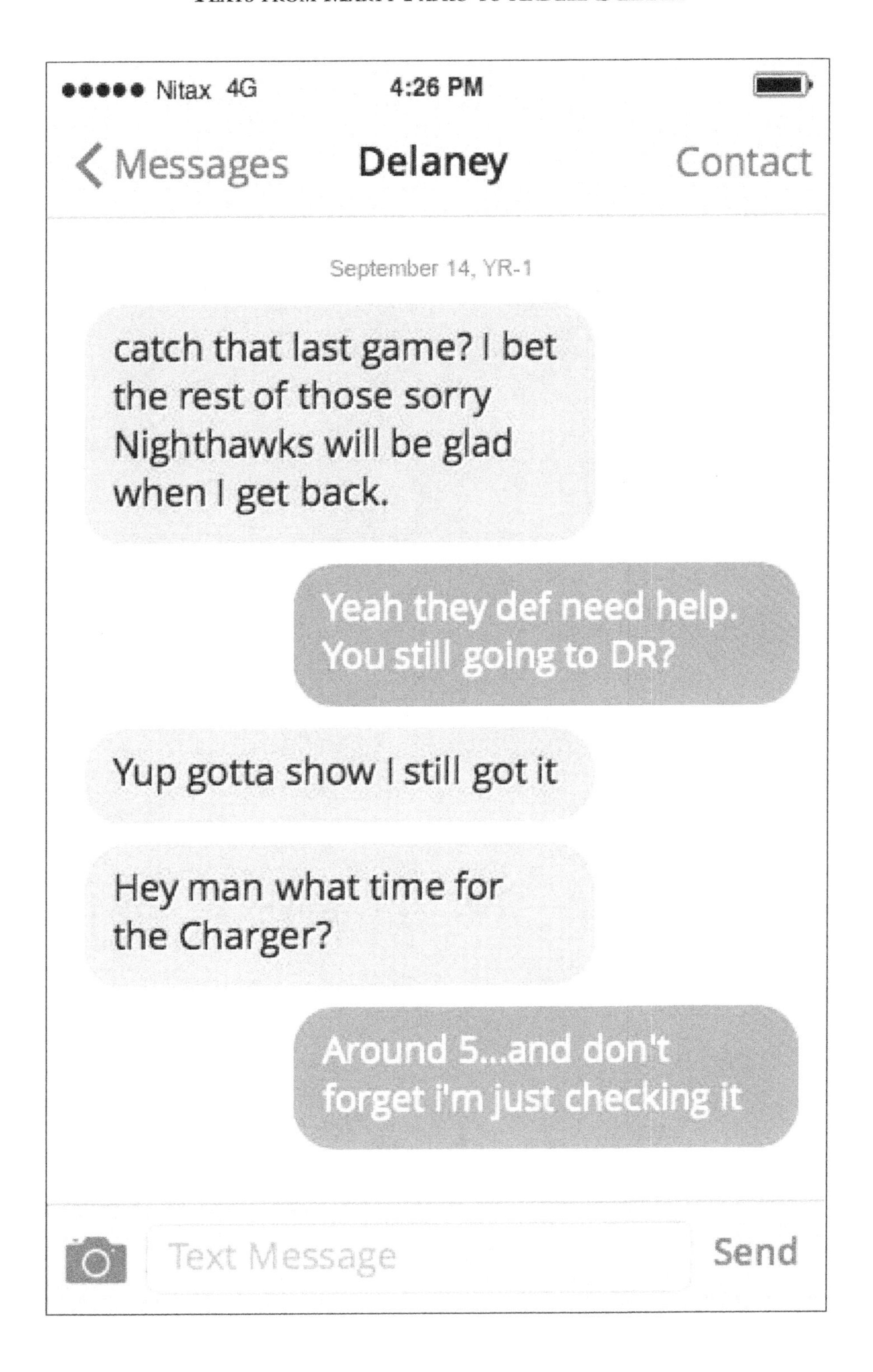

Exhibit 17

Police Seek Jewelry Store Gunman

Nita City, Nita - September 15: Miller's Fine Jewelry remains marked as a crime scene the morning after an armed robbery

By Jackson Benedict | The Press Clarion
Email the author | Follow on Twitter
on September 15, YR-1 at 8:57 AM

Police are seeking a lone gunman responsible for a late afternoon armed robbery of Miller's Fine Jewelry in the Pavilions. Detective Alex Lowrey of the Nita Police Department reported than an unmasked man entered the jewelry store about 5:30 yesterday afternoon and confronted Lexi Waitkus, the Assistant Manager. Lowrey said that Waitkus was ordered at gunpoint to the back of the store where the robber threatened to kill Waitkus unless he was given all the money. Waitkus complied and turned over all the cash, estimated to be around $25,000. Detective Lowrey said the incident was terrifying for Waitkus. Waitkus related that the gunman was very threatening, and that he also apparently boasted that he was making a "withdrawal" from the store.

Police have issued an all points bulletin for the suspect, described as armed and dangerous. He was described as a male in his twenties dressed in dark pants, a light tan jacket, and wearing a baseball cap. Detective Lowrey believes that there is sufficient evidence to expect a breakthrough before long. Lowrey said that the Nita Police Department has an excellent record of capturing suspects in such crimes. Lowrey would not comment on whether fingerprints had been recovered, but did say that the police had recovered some of the property taken that included currency, coins, and some silver dollars.

The Security Office of Pavilions was unavailable for comment, but Detective Lowrey said that security measures have been enhanced for all businesses at Pavilions, and special measures have been taken to ensure security at Miller's.

Exhibit 18

NITA CITY POLICE DEPARTMENT

3245 State Street
Nita City, NT 20235

283-555-2187
Fax: 283-555-2188

LINEUP FORM

You have been requested by the Nita City Police Department to attend an in-person lineup at the Darrow County Jail. The department appreciates your willingness to assist our department in the investigation of this case. In order to properly instruct you on the requirements for this procedure, we ask that you review the following:

1. The person who is suspected of this crime may or may not be present in the lineup. You should not assume just because the lineup is being conducted that the suspect in this case is present before you.

2. Please examine closely all the features of each of the subjects in the lineup before making any identification. The subjects will be asked to stand facing you, then to face to the right, and then to the left. At the conclusion of the lineup, each of the subjects will then leave the lineup room. If you require any additional time or wish any of the subjects to repeat any movements, simply make your request to the officer in charge of the lineup.

3. At the conclusion of the lineup, if you are able to make an identification, you should do so by writing below your identification and making any comments that you feel are appropriate describing your identification.

I WAS ____*x*____ WAS NOT ________ ABLE TO MAKE AN IDENTIFICATION.

IF YOU HAVE BEEN ABLE TO MAKE AN IDENTIFICATION, PLEASE ADD THE FOLLOWING:

I HAVE IDENTIFIED NUMBER < *4* > AS THE SUSPECT IN THIS CASE. I OFFER THE FOLLOWING COMMENTS CONCERNING MY IDENTIFICATION.

I think #4 is the person.

Signed: *Lexi Waitkus* Date: 9/22/YR-1

Witnessed: *Alex Lowery*

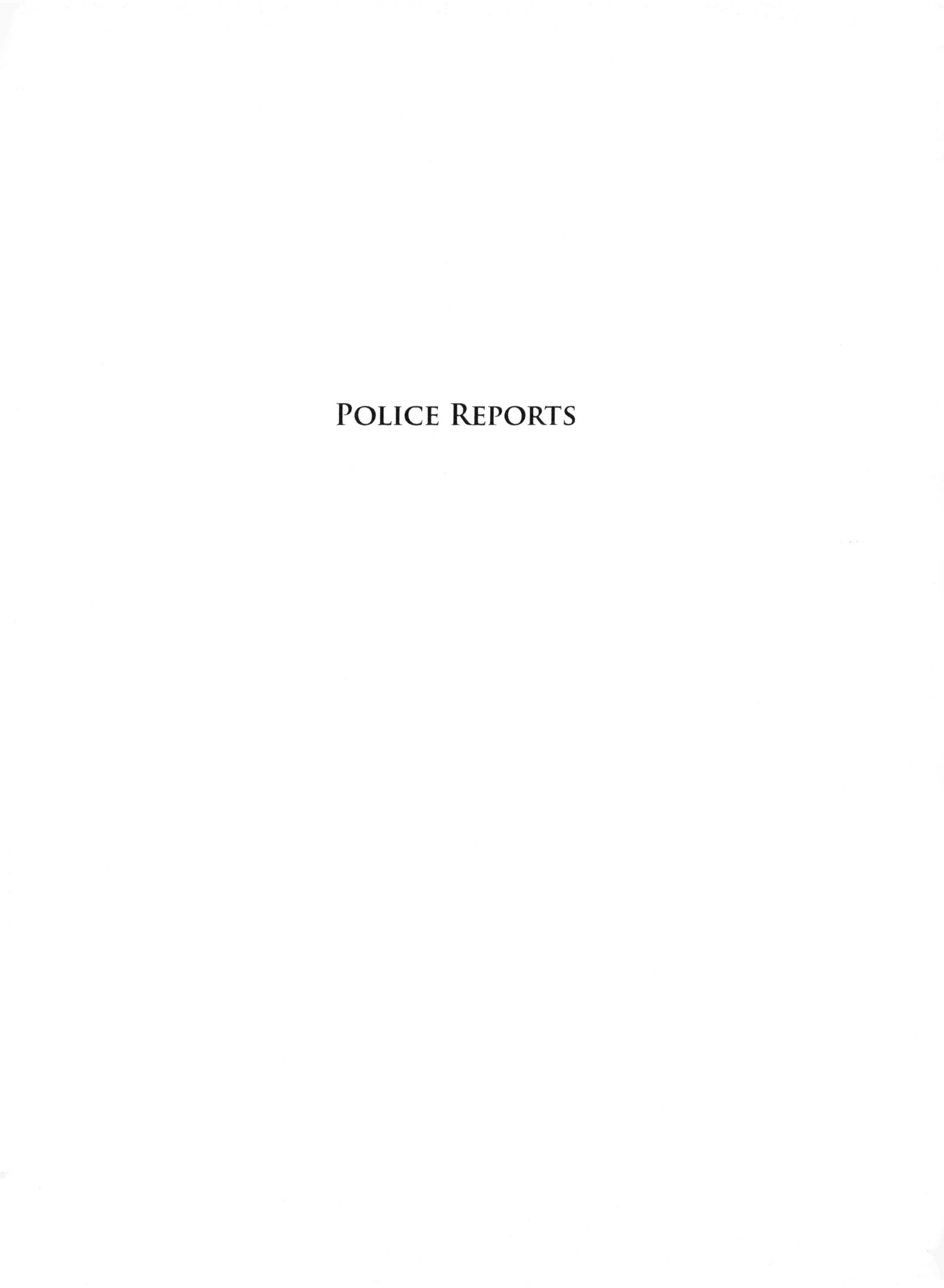

Police Reports

NITA CITY POLICE DEPARTMENT

3245 State Street
Nita City, NT 20235

283-555-2187
Fax: 283-555-2188

OFFENSE REPORT

FILE NUMBER:	YR-1-28117
VICTIM:	Lexi Waitkus 2994 E. Marshall Nita City, Nita
SUSPECT:	Unknown Male Adult Tan jacket, dark pants, baseball cap
LOCATION:	Miller's Fine Jewelers 29 Pavilions Plaza Nita City, Nita
OFFENSE:	CC 211—Armed Robbery
DATE OF REPORT:	September 14, YR-1
BY:	Detective Alex Lowrey AL Badge Number 212

Details of Offense: September 14, YR-1

FACTS:

At 1745 hours, I was concluding an interview of a witness in a homicide case when I received a radio call to go to Miller's Fine Jewelers at 29 Pavilions Plaza to meet with Officer Rickert and Lexi Waitkus concerning an armed robbery of Waitkus. I arrived at 1752 hours. Officer Rickert introduced me to Waitkus and Audie Passeau, and said that Waitkus had stopped Officer Rickert in Rickert's patrol car and reported that Waitkus had been robbed minutes before. I relieved Officer Rickert and took over the investigation of the case.

Waitkus appeared to be trembling and shaken from the experience. Waitkus informed me that an adult, **[specify race per Required Stipulation # 4]** male in his twenties took at gunpoint about $25,000 in cash and coins from the safe and fled. Waitkus said the male was dressed in a tan, waist-length jacket, had dark pants, and was wearing what looked like a baseball cap with the red and yellow logo. I immediately radioed the description to headquarters and asked that it be broadcast to all units in the northeast area.

I then began a close examination of the store and found an open safe in the store office. Several wrapped rolls of coins, two empty coin bags, checks, and a few bills were lying in and around the safe. I called for ID to send a technician to photograph the area and to dust for prints. At approximately 1810 hours, Supervising ID Technician Jan Nicholson arrived. Nicholson took several photos of the interior of Miller's and dusted the area of the safe, one of the jewelry counters, and the front door handle area.

I then made a check of adjacent businesses to see if anyone had seen a person of the description given by Waitkus, with negative results. I also looked in the immediate area to see if any of the currency or coins taken might have been dropped, and found nothing. I then returned to Miller's. Waitkus had calmed down somewhat, but was still understandably apprehensive. I then took a detailed statement from Waitkus.

STATEMENT OF LEXI WAITKUS

Waitkus is the Assistant Manager of Miller's Fine Jewelers. The store is in an upscale area of northwest Nita City and caters to clients with expensive tastes. Waitkus has worked there for three years and formerly worked for Ben Bridge Jewelers in the Downtown Mall. Waitkus said that usually there are at least two people at all times in Miller's. However, at about 1725 hours, Audie Passeau, a long-time clerk, had to pick up some newly purchased clothing from Nordstrom down the street and left through the front door. Waitkus was alone in the store and was preparing some of the store for closing at 1800 hours. About 1730 hours, the male subject entered and looked at several items. He seemed to be concentrating on men's watches. He then spoke to Waitkus and asked if Miller's had any sports watches. Waitkus informed him that in addition to the few they had on display, they had additional watches in the back room. The man said that he would like to see them.

Waitkus started to the back of the room and suddenly noticed the man alongside. The man said quietly, "Don't say anything. I have a gun." Waitkus looked and saw that the man had what looked like a dark revolver in his right hand. The gun was pointed down. The man then said, "I want the money, not the jewelry. Get all the money now, or I'll kill you. Do you understand?" Waitkus nodded and walked to the back of the office, where the safe is located. The money and checks are kept there. The safe is regulated by a combination lock. Waitkus told the man that the safe was locked, and he said, "You had better hope that you can open it. Otherwise, you're out." The man made a motion throwing his left hand and thumb up like an umpire's movement. Waitkus knew the combination, opened the safe, and stood aside. The man grabbed one of the coin bags and then began stuffing bills and coins in the bag. Some of the coins included five silver dollars that were going to be mounted on key chains for a client. The man then told Waitkus to lie down on the office floor and remain there for fifteen minutes. He said that if Waitkus moved, he would be watching and come back and kill Waitkus. Waitkus lay down on the floor. The man left, walking toward the front door. About five minutes later Passeau came in and found Waitkus. Waitkus was shaking uncontrollably but was able to call 911 and report the robbery. Waitkus was able to get a good look at the suspect despite the fact that the baseball cap was pulled down over much of the upper portion of the face.

I asked Waitkus what security measures Miller's has. Waitkus said there is a Pavilions security company for all of the Pavilions businesses. I asked Waitkus if Miller's has security cameras, and Waitkus said they have three security cameras mounted on the ceiling in the main room. Waitkus did not review any of the recordings. They had a problem on one previous incident where a customer complained about rude conduct by a previous employee, and on that occasion they were unable to retrieve any video recording. There were memory cards that apparently were incorrectly formatted. Waitkus said they would check immediately, but they would need the boss to handle that. Waitkus said the man was wearing the baseball cap which was slightly pulled down over the top of his forehead, but Waitkus could clearly see most of the man's face.

Waitkus assured me that the store would complete an inventory of the missing money, coins, and any other property that might have been taken and would report that to me. I informed Waitkus that the department would continue the investigation, including checking out the physical description, the clothing, and any fingerprints that we might be able to lift. Waitkus assured me of their complete cooperation in the case, but expressed again great fear of the suspect and asked if there was anything we could do to offer protection. I said that I would bring the matter to the attention of the lieutenant in charge as well as the private security company that patrols Pavilions Plaza. I further explained to Waitkus that my department would need the security recordings as soon as possible.

FURTHER INVESTIGATION

In examining the store, I noticed that the interior was well lit. This was true in the main showroom as well as the office where the safe was located. I then checked with Supervising ID Technician Nicholson, who informed me that Nicholson was able to recover two prints from the inside top area of the safe. Nicholson and I then left the shop and walked east and then south down Pavilions Plaza in order to take a scene photo. When we got to Number 35, approximately 180 feet from Miller's, I noticed a cloth coin bag in the gutter. I picked it up, saw that it read "1,000 dimes," and saw one silver dollar in the bottom. We returned to Miller's. I asked Waitkus to look at the bag and at the silver dollar without touching the coin. Waitkus examined both and said that the bag appeared to be one of Miller's, as Waitkus remembered the "1,000 dimes" being written on the side. Waitkus could see that the silver dollar bore the date 1900 and said that was one of the dates of the coins, but Waitkus would have to check their records for more precise information. I gave the bag to Supervising ID Technician Nicholson and asked that the silver dollar in the bag also be examined for possible prints. Nicholson and I then returned to the station.

At approximately 1850 hours, Waitkus called me at the station and reported that Passeau and Waitkus had conducted an exact inventory of the cash and currency in the safe and that $22,440 was missing. That included the five silver dollars with the dates 1882, 1883, 1889, 1900, and 1903. Waitkus said the silver dollar that was recovered was identical to the 1900 that was missing.

NITA CITY POLICE DEPARTMENT

3245 State Street
Nita City, NT 20235

283-555-2187
Fax: 283-555-2188

SUPPLEMENTAL OFFENSE REPORT

FILE NO.: YR-1-28117

SUSPECT: Unknown Male Adult
Tan jacket, dark pants, baseball cap

LOCATION: Miller's Fine Jewelers
29 Pavilions Plaza
Nita City, Nita

OFFENSES: C.C. 211—Armed Robbery

DATE OF REPORT: September 15, YR-1

BY: Detective Alex Lowrey AL
Badge Number # 212

SUPPLEMENTAL INFORMATION OF IDENTITY OF SUSPECT

At 1130 hours on September 15, YR-1, I received a call from Waitkus who informed me that Waitkus and the owner of Miller's Fine Jewelry, Dom Dallessandro, examined the PTZ security cameras and the memory cards. The capture system failed to record footage. This apparently was the same problem they had previously. Waitkus said that there was no actual film in the system. Waitkus said that Dallesandro was very upset and said that the camera system would not ever be used again, and he said that he would have a completely new system that would never again have this problem.

I checked with our media unit and was informed that PTZ—that is, pan-tilt-zoom—cameras now record on memory cards in capture systems, rather than actual film in the camera itself. If these memory cards have not been formatted properly—that is, cleared of previous content or changed to the appropriate file system used by the capture system—then the capture system may produce an error and fail to record footage as it normally would.

Nita City Police Department

3245 State Street
Nita City, NT 20235

283-555-2187
Fax: 283-555-2188

OFFENSE REPORT

FILE NO.:	YR-1-28243
SUSPECT:	Val Cavarretta 110 E. Wyse Street # 7 Nita City, Nita
LOCATION:	Broadway and 21st Street Nita City, Nita
OFFENSES:	C.C. 11351—Possession for Sale of Cocaine N.V.C. 23152a—DUI Alcohol
DATE OF REPORT:	September 21, YR-1
BY:	Officer Alicia Johnson AJ #172 Badge Number # 172

Details of Offenses

At 1931 hours, I was on routine patrol in the area of Broadway and Twenty-First Street. I was northbound in the center lane of Twenty-First Street, a one-way, three-lane street and saw a YR-7 dark Chevrolet with darkened windows approximately 200 feet ahead in the same lane. It was weaving beyond the borders of the lane and on several occasions slowed without any perceptible reason and then quickly accelerated. I activated my warning lights and pulled the car over to the east curb of Twenty-First Street about one-half block north of Broadway. As I approached the driver's window, which was also darkened, the driver rolled the window down and said, "Hey, officer, I didn't do anything. What's the problem?" I could smell an alcohol odor on the driver's breath. I asked for identification and the driver presented an expired Nita license bearing the name of Val Cavarretta. I asked Cavarretta to exit the car in order to perform some field sobriety tests. Cavarretta started to get out of the car and pushed an item into the crack of the car seat. From my position, I could not tell if it was a weapon, so I immediately retrieved it and saw that what appeared to me to resemble about a half-key, or half-kilo, of a white powdery substance, probably cocaine. Cavarretta immediately said, "Hey, I don't know whose that is."

I gave Cavarretta a standard battery of three field sobriety tests: the finger-to-nose test, the counting backwards test, and the heel-to-toe test. Cavarretta failed all three tests. I then placed Cavarretta under arrest for suspicion of both CC 11351 (Possession for Sale of Cocaine) and CC

23152 (Misdemeanor Driving Under the Influence of Alcohol). Cavarretta was then taken to the Nita County Jail and refused to give a breath, blood, or urine test. Cavarretta said that I should get in touch with detectives and ask them to come talk, as Cavarretta had something for them that they might want to hear.

I then notified Detective Alex Lowrey, who took over the matter.

NITA CITY POLICE DEPARTMENT

3245 State Street
Nita City, NT 20235

283-555-2187
Fax: 283-555-2188

BUREAU OF IDENTIFICATION FINGERPRINT REPORT

FILE NO.:	YR-1-28117
SUSPECT:	Ardell Patrick Delaney 1215 Lake Chipman Drive #298 Nita City, Nita
LOCATION:	Miller's Fine Jewelers 29 Pavilions Plaza Nita City, Nita
OFFENSES:	C.C. 211—Armed Robbery
DATE OF REPORT:	September 22, YR-1
BY:	Supervising ID Technician Jan Nicholson JN

Per the request of dispatch, on September 14, YR-1, at approximately 1810 hours, I responded to 29 Pavilions Plaza in Nita City to assist Detective Alex Lowrey at the scene. I was asked by Det. Lowrey to photograph the scene and to dust for possible prints in the area of the safe and the entrance doorway. I took several photos of the interior of Miller's Fine Jewelry. I inspected the area of the doorway and did not detect any prints. I then inspected the area of the safe. Inside the safe, approximately two inches below the top, I observed and lifted two impressions, which I labeled Latent #1. I checked the area of the counter where Lexi Waitkus had first seen the suspect and found no prints.

Shortly thereafter, Detective Lowrey and I left the store and walked east and then south on Pavilions Plaza. I took a scene photo showing Miller's. Detective Lowrey found a cloth bag in the gutter nearby, and in inspecting the bag found a silver dollar. We returned to Miller's, and Detective Lowrey showed the bag and dollar to the Assistant Manager, Lexi Waitkus, who identified the bag and said the dollar appeared similar to one that had been at Miller's. I took custody of both items and transported them to the station. There, I opened the cloth bag, carefully removed the 1900 silver dollar, and processed it for prints. I was able to find one usable latent, which I lifted and labeled Latent #2. I booked both Latents #1 and #2 as evidence in my evidence locker. The bag did not lend itself to latent print retention and was not dusted for prints.

On September 22, YR-1, at about 0940 hours, Detective Lowrey contacted me by phone and asked me to compare department prints of Ardell Delaney with the latent prints in this case. I told Lowrey I would do so. I then obtained the official print records of Ardell Patrick Delaney and compared them with the lifted Latents #1 and #2 that I recovered in this case. The results were inconclusive, although I did find seven points of comparison between Latent # 2 and the department print of Delaney's left index finger.

I returned Latents #1 and #2 to my evidence locker. I then called Detective Lowrey at approximately 1045 hours and informed Detective Lowrey of the results. Detective Lowrey asked if my examination of Latent #2 was a positive match, and I informed Detective Lowrey that I could not say so.

NITA CITY POLICE DEPARTMENT

3245 State Street
Nita City, NT 20235

283-555-2187
Fax: 283-555-2188

SUPPLEMENTAL OFFENSE REPORT

FILE NO.:	YR-1-28117
SUSPECT:	Ardell Patrick Delaney 1215 Lake Chipman Drive # 298 Nita City, Nita
LOCATION:	Miller's Fine Jewelers 29 Pavilions Plaza Nita City, Nita
OFFENSES:	C.C. 211—Armed Robbery
DATE OF REPORT:	September 25, YR-1
BY:	Detective Alex Lowrey AL Badge Number # 212

SUPPLEMENTAL INFORMATION OF IDENTITY OF SUSPECT

At 2115 hours on September 21, YR-1, I was notified by Officer Johnson that Johnson had arrested a Val Cavarretta for possession for sale of cocaine and DUI. Officer Johnson said that Cavarretta wanted to reveal some information about a major case in exchange for consideration on Cavarretta's present charges. I informed Johnson that I would speak with Cavarretta in the county jail in a few minutes.

At approximately 2145 hours on the same day, I met with Cavarretta at the County Jail. I informed Cavarretta fully of the Miranda rights. Cavarretta responded by saying, "I know my rights. I don't want to talk about my case. I want to talk about another case. I know the police are looking for the fellow who robbed the jewelry store out at Pavilions. I can give you some information, but I don't want to say anything until I know what you're going to do for me."

I told Cavarretta that I would need to do some checking, and then I would make contact again. I then left and returned to the detective division and spoke with Lieutenant Meers, the lieutenant on duty. Lieutenant Meers was familiar with the Miller's Jewelry case. I informed Lieutenant Meers that we did not have any further leads on the suspect although the robbery case occurred one week ago. Lieutenant Meers authorized me to tell Cavarretta that we had to have the information, we had to check its accuracy, and then if we felt the information was good, we would tell Cavarretta what we could do on Cavarretta's charges before we used the information. I was to tell Cavarretta that we promised not to use any of the information unless and until there was an agreement.

I then returned to the County Jail and informed Cavarretta of the terms. Cavarretta agreed to talk and gave me the following information:

Cavarretta went to Poly High in Nita City. Cavarretta got into some trouble and was on juvenile probation. Ardell Delaney was also going to Poly High and also on juvenile probation, and they worked in the same work crews. They became friends. Delaney went on to become a top pitcher for Poly's baseball team, won All-League, then All-State, and then went to University of Nita, where he was a star athlete. He got pro offers. Delaney joined the Nita City Nighthawks farm system. Cavarretta had not seen Delaney since high school, other than to say hello from time to time. He did see Delaney's picture in the paper and saw sports articles about him. He lost contact with Delaney until earlier this year.

Sometime around July, Cavarretta was at a rock concert and saw Delaney. They chatted. Delaney said that he had hurt his arm throwing without warming up properly and had to go on the disabled list. Delaney knew that Cavarretta used to smoke dope, so Delaney asked Cavarretta where he could get some good stuff. Cavarretta asked what kind of stuff, and Delaney said he wasn't talking weed. He wanted some good coke. He said that he had used coke off and on at Gulfport, someplace in Iowa, and when they had winter ball in the Dominican Republic. Cavarretta promised to check it out and let Delaney know. Delaney said that he could be reached at some auto repair shop, just talk to Marty. Delaney gave Cavarretta the phone number, but Cavarretta no longer has it.

Cavarretta made contact with a fellow they call Duke. Duke said that a half-key was fifteen grand and that he could get it on two days' notice. Cavarretta then texted Marty, who said Delaney would call Cavarretta back. Later that day, Delaney called, and Cavarretta said a half-key would be sixteen grand. Delaney said he would have to see what he could do about the money and would get back to Cavarretta. That was the last Cavarretta heard from Delaney until last week. Cavarretta got a call from Delaney, and Delaney said, "Remember the deal we talked about. I'm ready. I had to make a little withdrawal from an account I had at a jewelry store." Delaney then laughed. Cavarretta said that would be OK, but it would take a couple of days to put it together. Cavarretta contacted Duke, and because Cavarretta and Duke had a relationship of trust, Duke gave the dope to Cavarretta with the promise of the fifteen grand in two days. Cavarretta was driving home with the half-key when the arrest took place. Cavarretta never got the chance to call Delaney.

Cavarretta heard through the grapevine that Delaney made pretty good money when he was playing ball, but after the arm injury, Delaney had gone through all the money he had saved and was still using dope. The word was that Delaney was getting desperate for money and that Delaney's landlord was going to evict him soon. Delaney apparently lived in an upscale apartment or condo area near Lake Chipman.

Cavarretta expressed great concern about what might happen since Cavarretta had not paid Duke. I asked Cavarretta to agree to make the call to Delaney to set up the deal, and Nita PD would wire Cavarretta and record the transaction on video. Cavarretta said, "No way. I'll give you the information, but I'm not going up front like that." I told Cavarretta that we could try and make the case with the identification by the victim of the robbery, but I could not promise that the defense lawyer wouldn't find out about Cavarretta through court discovery. Cavarretta understood that was possible and said if that happened that Cavarretta would just live with that, but would not go through a setup. I told Cavarretta that I would recommend that if the victim was able to identify Delaney, and if the DA agreed to file charges on the case after a lineup, then we would ask the DA to agree to recommend probation on his charges. Cavarretta agreed.

FINGERPRINT INFORMATION FROM SUPERVISING ID TECHNICIAN NICHOLSON

On September 22, YR-1, at approximately 0945 hours, I checked with Supervising ID Technician Jan Nicholson, who informed me that the fingerprint check of the 1900 silver dollar revealed one usable print. I asked Nicholson to check department records for the print of Ardell Delaney and to inform me of the results. Nicholson called me back at approximately 1050 hours and reported that a check of the prints on file for Delaney revealed that there were seven points of similarity on the silver dollar print to that of Delaney's left index finger. Nicholson said that the dollar surface was not favorable for good prints, and generally fingerprint experts require eight points for a positive identification, but in Nicholson's opinion seven points indicate that the print is consistent with Delaney touching the dollar.

EFFORTS TO SET UP IN-PERSON LINEUP

Lieutenant Meers and I discussed the question of whether Ardell Delaney should be arrested on probable cause, and decided that we should first determine whether Lexi Waitkus could identify Delaney. We made the decision to arrange a lineup. I conferred by phone with Deputy District Attorney Aaron Grimm, who advised that we would need an order signed by a judge authorizing taking Delaney into limited custody for the purpose of a lineup. I informed Mr. Grimm that we wanted to set up the lineup for that afternoon, September 22, and wanted to contact Delaney as soon as possible. Mr. Grimm arranged for Judge Landis to review the case to determine whether the order should issue. At 1115 hours, Mr. Grimm and I met with Judge Landis, and I related under oath the information set out above, including the statement of Cavarretta, the findings of Supervising ID Technician Nicholson, and the similarity in description of Delaney. Judge Landis issued the order.

On September 22, YR-1, at approximately 1145 hours, I made arrangements with the sheriff's department at the county jail to select five subjects fitting the description of Delaney for a lineup that afternoon at approximately 1530 hours. I then drove from the station to the Lake Chipman area, about four miles from downtown and about the same distance from Miller's Fine Jewelers. Since I had worked the area both as a patrol officer and later as a detective, I knew that there were three main apartment complexes, all at the west end of the lake. I began checking Lakeshore Apartments at 1215 Lake Chipman Drive and discovered the name Delaney listed at apartment 298. I then called dispatch and asked for a covering officer. Dispatch responded that Officer Johnson was on duty and would respond. Officer Johnson arrived at approximately 1215 hours. We then went to apartment 298, rang the bell, and Ardell Delaney answered. He was in his swimsuit, said that he had just done a few laps, and asked that we wait until he dried off. After changing, he came back to his living room.

I told Delaney that I was investigating a reported robbery and that in the course of the investigation we developed evidence pointing to the possibility of his being the robber. I informed him that Judge Landis had issued a court order authorizing us to take him into limited custody for the purpose of conducting a lineup and that we intended to hold the lineup that afternoon. He said he was dumbfounded that the police would think he might be involved and wanted to know what this was all about. I told him that I was not at liberty to give him any details now and repeated that we simply wanted to complete the lineup. He asked what would happen if he refused. I said that based on the court order, he had no right to refuse. We then went to the station, where we arrived at approximately 1300 hours. I left Delaney in the custody of Officer Johnson.

I then called Miller's Fine Jewelers and spoke to Audie Passeau, who put Lexi Waitkus on the line. Waitkus agreed to come to a lineup scheduled that afternoon at 1530 hours. I then returned to the station.

THE LINEUP

On September 22, YR-1, at approximately 1530 hours, I met with Lexi Waitkus at the station. I informed Waitkus that the person who committed the robbery might or might not be in the lineup and that Waitkus was simply to look at each of the men, and then when the lineup was over, Waitkus should write down on the lineup form what, if any, identification was made. Waitkus agreed. At 1545 hours in the lineup room of the Darrow County Jail, I conducted the lineup with six male subjects, including Ardell Delaney, who was in position number four. Each of the subjects was of the same race, the same age group, and within two inches in height and ten pounds in weight of the others. None had any distinctive facial markings. Each man was dressed in the orange overalls issued by the county jail. I asked each of the males to stand facing forward, then turn to the right, and then turn to the left. The lighting in the viewing room was reasonably dark, and the lineup room, displaying the six subjects, was very well lit. The subjects in the lineup could not see anyone in the viewing room because of the one-way glass and the lighting.

Waitkus spent several minutes viewing the lineup then nodded to me, and I terminated the lineup. Waitkus completed the lineup form and wrote, *I think # 4 is the person.* I thanked Waitkus and said that we would be in touch about the case. I then released the other five subjects in the lineup. I then conferred with Lieutenant Meers, and we agreed that Ardell Delaney should be arrested on probable cause. I placed Delaney under arrest for robbery of the first degree and asked Ardell Delaney to accompany me to the detective division.

STATEMENT OF ARDELL DELANEY

At approximately 1615 hours, I met with Ardell Delaney in an interview room at the detective division. I informed Delaney again that he was under arrest and then fully advised him of his Miranda rights. I told him that I wanted to discuss a robbery of a jewelry store. He said that he would talk to me about the matter, that he had nothing to hide, and that he was completely innocent. He said that this was a big mistake. I described briefly the details of the robbery, telling Delaney the date, time, and location and a brief summary of the facts of the case. Delaney said that he only knew vaguely of the matter from an article on the *Press Clarion* website last week. I then told him that we had reliable information that he was the robber, that he matched the description, and that he had been identified by the victim. Delaney repeated that this was a big mistake. He denied ever being at the store. He said that the only jewelry store he had been to in Nita City in the last year was Ben Bridge in the Downtown Mall, sometime in June, to look at watches.

Delaney said that in thinking about what he did on the evening of September 14, he thinks that afternoon he had his car inspected for a emissions certificate. The shop was at the other end of town, in the southeast sector. His friend Marty owns the shop. Delaney denied using cocaine or any dope. He said that his whole life is baseball, and he would never do anything to mess that up, as he believes that he has a very promising career. He had progressed through the minor leagues playing in Gulfport and Cedar Rapids and winter ball in the Dominican Republic. He injured his pitching arm and just has to complete his shoulder therapy. He expects to be playing winter ball this year. He said that the coaches have told him that he is ready for major league ball, depending on the results of winter ball.

I asked Delaney if he minded if our department searched his apartment and his car. He asked what would happen if he refused. I said that we would seek a search warrant, and if the court gave us one, we would then conduct the search. He then said he had no objections as long as he could accompany us and as long as he could make a call to arrange for bail. I told him that he was entitled to make such a confidential call. I completed the interview. Delaney was allowed to make the call. We then drove to the Lakeshore Apartments. Again, Officer Johnson acted as a covering officer. Delaney let us into the apartment. I promised him that we would leave his apartment in the same condition as we found it. We then conducted a search of the master bedroom, the second smaller bedroom, the kitchen, living room, and the patio. We did not find any currency, rolled coins, coin wrappers, checks, silver dollars, coin bags, handguns, or ammunition. In the course of conducting the search, I asked Delaney if he had any silver dollars. He said no, and then asked why that was important. I told him that silver dollars were taken in the robbery. I did find a baseball cap with the logo of the Nighthawks, which Delaney said was his from playing with the Nighthawks in spring training. I took custody of the cap. I noticed that the logo on the cap is red and yellow and looks like a wing. We then went to the garage, where his YR-2 Dodge Charger SRT8 was parked. Officer Johnson and I searched it with negative results. Officer Johnson and I then returned to the station with Delaney.

At the station, I informed Delaney that I was going to book him at the Darrow County Jail. I then walked over to the jail. During the booking process, Delaney said that he had more time to think about the case and had more information he wanted to pass on to us. He believed that if we looked carefully at the case, we would see that he was not guilty. I told him that I would be happy to talk further with him, and after the booking process was completed, I then took Delaney to an interview room in the county jail.

ADDITIONAL STATEMENT FROM ARDELL DELANEY

At approximately 1815 hours, Ardell Delaney said that he was sure that in the late afternoon of September 14, he was having his Dodge Charger SRT8 checked for emissions by Marty Pafko. He said that he realized that since Pafko did not complete the process and that he would have to take his car to an authorized Dodge dealer, there was no charge and no paperwork. He said that Pafko can corroborate his whereabouts. I asked him how I would get in touch with Pafko, and he said that Marty's Repairs is listed in the book.

Delaney said that he thought more about his visit to Ben Bridge and remembered looking at a silver dollar. The clerk told him that silver dollars were plated with gold and made into key chains or pendants. He looked at several silver dollars but decided against the idea.

Delaney asked why the police first suspected that he might be involved and said that if anybody suggested he was involved, that person was a liar and was making a big mistake. He said that he was going to call the Nighthawks, and they would get the best lawyers in town, and people would be sorry they falsely accused him. I repeated what I had told him earlier: that we had reliable information that he was the robber, and he had been identified by the victim.

I told Delaney that our department records reflected three crimes of theft in the past. Delaney said that he wanted to explain about his past. He said that about seven years ago, when he was about sixteen, he and a couple of friends from school got into an argument with another student about money the other student owed his friend. They held the student down and took the exact amount of money owed, and the other student called the cops. He went to juvenile court, and his lawyer, a public defender, told him he had better plead guilty for twenty days in juvenile hall, or he could go to the Darrow County Youth Authority if he denied it and went to trial.

He said that about eight months later, he and a friend got drunk, and as sort of a high school prank, they went into a garage and took a bicycle, which they rode double down the street. They were only going to "borrow" the bike to get to school when the cops caught them and took them to juvenile hall. He said that his lawyer told him that because the garage was attached to the house, it was burglary first degree. Delaney said they fought it and went to trial about two weeks later, and the judge found him guilty. This time, they put him in juvenile hall for three months. He said that he hated juvenile hall, although they let him out early so he could rejoin his high school class and play ball that spring. He said he was determined not to do anything stupid like that ever again.

Then four years ago, as an adult, he was in his third year at University of Nita. The baseball team had just finished a game against Iowa State. He went to a drugstore somewhere in Ames, Iowa, to pick up some items and left, forgetting to pay for the items. He went to court that day, and the attorney they gave him said that if he pled guilty, he would get straight probation and a fine. I asked Delaney why the court would do that with his record, and he said that the judge in Iowa didn't have his juvenile record. He was allowed to pay off the $400 fine over two years. I then concluded the interview, and said that I would arrange for him to call a lawyer, and took him to the booking desk, where the booking sergeant made those arrangements.

I took the baseball cap to the ID Section and Supervising ID Tech. Nicholson photographed the cap. I retained custody of the cap in my evidence locker.

On September 24, YR-1, at approximately 0945 hours, I delivered the entire case to the District Attorney's Office and met with Deputy DA Aaron Grimm. Grimm agreed that there was sufficient evidence to prosecute the case but said that it was imperative that the DA's Office contact the attorney for Val Cavarretta to secure the testimony of Cavarretta. Grimm said their office would take care of the matter and would contact me. DA Grimm called me back at approximately 1115 and said that Cavarretta would agree to testify in exchange for straight probation with no jail time. I told Grimm that our department backed such an agreement. Grimm then assured me that the DA's Office would file a complaint.

FURTHER INVESTIGATION

At approximately 1650 hours, by phone I contacted Ben Bridge Jewelers at Downtown Mall and spoke with the manager, Angie McCullough. I asked if they ever carried silver dollars. She said they sometimes have them in stock, and she thought they had a few at the present time. I asked if she knew whether they carried any around June of YR-1. She said there would be no way of knowing and no records. I asked if they were gold plated and used for key chains. She said that was occasionally done. I asked her if there was any way of tracking any silver dollars that they might have had back in June. She said there was not. I then asked her if they could have transferred them or traded them to Miller's Fine Jewelers. She said that might be possible but unlikely. She said that clerks sometimes liked to collect them, and a clerk might have exchanged one for a paper dollar and then later used it. She said that she would ask the two clerks and the jeweler and would call me back to let me know what information, if any, she could discover.

At approximately 1730 hours, I called Lexi Waitkus and asked if there was any possibility that one of the silver dollars taken in the robbery could have been received earlier in the year from Ben Bridge in Downtown Mall. Waitkus said that Waitkus maintains fairly frequent contact with former coworkers from Ben Bridge but doesn't recall getting any silver dollars from them. However, silver dollars are occasionally picked up at a trade show if there is a specific need. Waitkus believes that the silver dollars they had on hand came from a trade show, and they paid wholesale price for them. Waitkus said there are no records from the trade show, only the inventory records showing what they had on hand.

On September 25, YR-1, at 1050 hours, I received a call from Angie McCullough of Ben Bridge who said further checking did not reveal any more information from the two clerks or the jeweler. McCullough said that they may have disposed of silver dollars in the past at trade shows, but she does not recall doing so, and they have no records of any such transactions.

On September 25, YR-1, at 1130 hours, I checked Google and found Marty's Auto Repairs at 3914 Dallesandro Way. I called and spoke with Marty Pafko. I informed Pafko of Delaney's arrest and asked if I could come by and speak with Pafko. Pafko agreed. Marty's Auto Repair is approximately eight miles from Miller's Fine Jewelry. I asked Pafko if Pafko had conducted an emissions exam of Delaney's car. Pafko said sometime around a week or so ago Delaney came by and said he had a problem "smogging" his car. Pafko assumed Delaney meant getting it approved by the Department of Motor Vehicles. Pafko looked at the car and saw that one of the valves seemed to have been tampered with, and Pafko knew this would be a problem. Pafko then suggested Delaney take it to an authorized dealer for proper repairs. Pafko said there was no paperwork, and Pafko could not remember what date it was. I concluded the interview. Later, at the station, I ran an automated record check on Pafko and saw that Pafko was on probation for a charge of pocketing money of illegal aliens, who were trying to send the money to a foreign country.

NITA CITY POLICE DEPARTMENT

3245 State Street
Nita City, NT 20235

283-555-2187
Fax: 283-555-2188

SUPPLEMENTAL OFFENSE REPORT

FILE NO.: YR-1-28117

SUSPECT: Ardell Patrick Delaney
1215 Lake Chipman Drive # 298
Nita City, Nita

LOCATION: Miller's Fine Jewelers
29 Pavilions Plaza
Nita City, Nita

OFFENSES: C.C. 211—Armed Robbery

DATE OF REPORT: September 27, YR-1

BY: Detective Alex Lowrey AL
Badge Number # 212

SUPPLEMENTAL INFORMATION OF IDENTITY OF SUSPECT

At 0915 hours on September 26, YR-1, I received a call from Val Cavarretta, who was at the county jail. Cavarretta asked that we talk about "the case" and said that there was some more information about the case, and asked that we talk at the jail. At 1014 hours, I met Cavarretta at the jail interview room, and Cavarretta told me that there was more information identifying Delaney as the robber. Cavarretta said there was corroboration in a page of Cavarretta's Facebook in a post about having some "Aunt Nora," which is a street name for cocaine, and in another post about running into Delaney at a Nasties concert. Cavarretta agreed to present me with those posts and agreed I could use them to support Cavarretta's account of the sale. Cavarretta said I would find them in his Samsung cell phone, and offered to authorize me to retrieve the phone at the front desk and bring it back to the interview room and show me the Facebook pages.

I then went to the booking desk, obtained the phone, and returned to the interview room. Cavarretta first showed me the Facebook Event Page about the Nasties concert. The "Insights" box on the right-hand side of the page displayed information about who attended the concert. The section shows both Cavarretta's and Delaney's profile pictures. This is a public Facebook page, accessible to anyone on the internet.

Cavarretta then showed me a screenshot from Cavarretta's personal Facebook page. There are several posts of interest on this page. The topmost post seems to reflect Cavarretta making reference to being in possession of cocaine, as "Aunt Nora" is a street name for this substance. The second post seems to reflect Cavarretta making mention of his running into Delaney at the Nasties concert. The third post is an article that Cavarretta shared from the *Press Clarion* website indicating and corroborating that Cavarretta does sometimes read the *Press Clarion*. This page would be private to everyone except Cavarretta and those whom Cavarretta has friended on Facebook, and clearly Cavarretta has shared this page with our department. As a result of my viewing Cavarretta's cell phone, I asked for and received Cavarretta's permission to print this Facebook page. I took the cell phone to the sheriff's booking office and printed the page and later booked the page in evidence at the police station.

On September 27, YR-1, at 1340 hours, I called Marty Pafko and asked if Pafko had at any time contacted Delaney by Facebook regarding this matter, and if so, I asked if Pafko would share that information. Pafko said there was nothing in particular, but we would be authorized to look at any of Pafko's Facebook pages information on Pafko's Facebook page. At 1420 hours, I met Pafko at Marty's Auto Repair. Pafko took me to the office and brought up Pafko's Facebook page and, since Pafko is one of Delaney's Facebook friends, Pafko navigated to a screenshot from Delaney's personal Facebook page. There are several posts of interest on this page. The topmost post seems to suggest that Delaney was dealing with car emissions issues. The second post reflects Delaney complaining about his shoulder pain just a few weeks before the robbery. The fourth post could be taken as Delaney's commenting on good drugs being available in the Dominican Republic. I asked if Pafko would share this page with our department and print a copy that I could take to department. Pafko agreed, printed the page, and handed it to me. I returned to the station and logged in the printed Facebook page as evidence in the case.

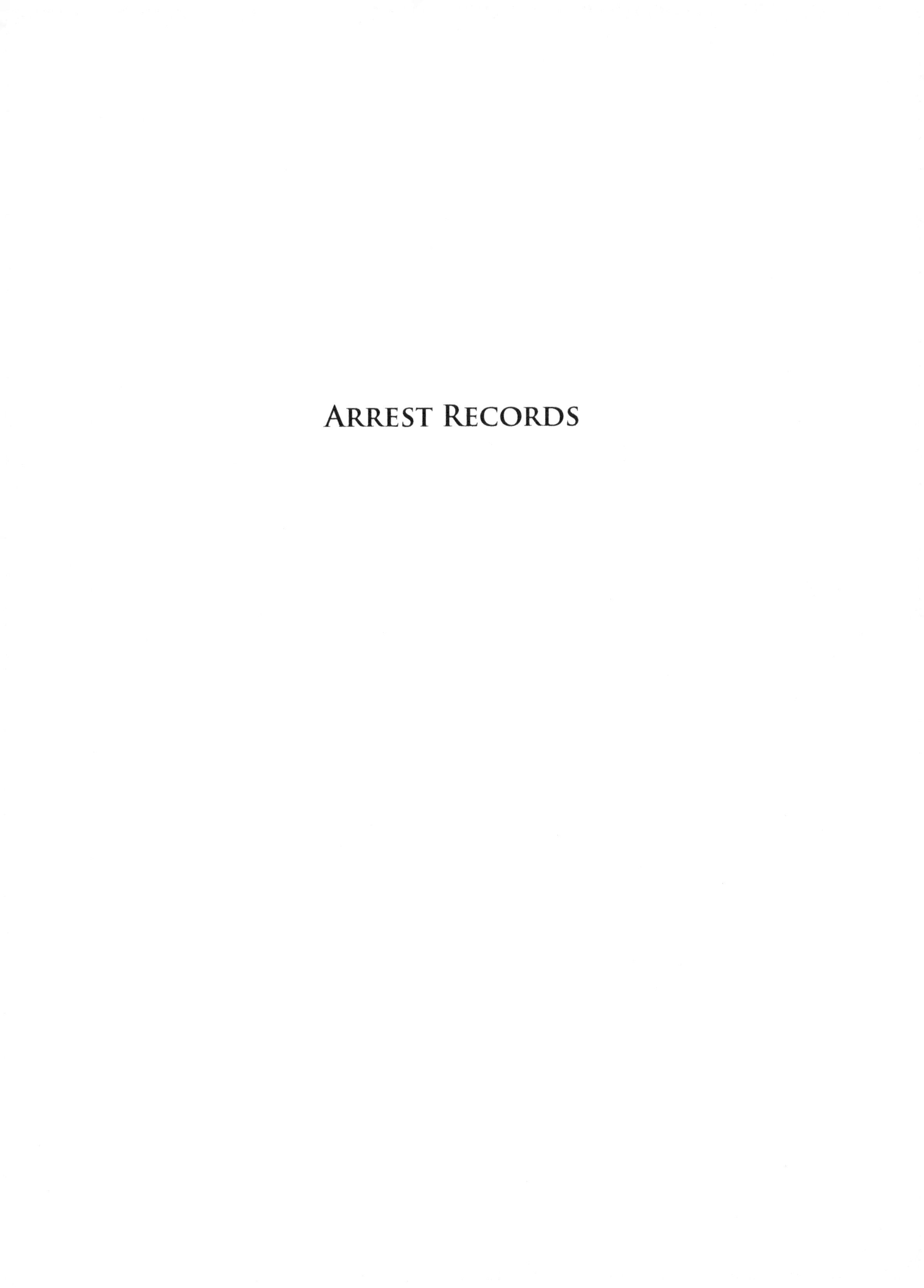

Arrest Records

ARREST AND CONVICTION RECORD OF ARDELL PATRICK DELANEY

RE: FOX, M. DCDA DATE: 09-24-YR-1 TIME: 1632

CIR/C9354718

DOB/06-23-YR-24

SEX/M

NAM/01 DELANEY, ARDELL PATRICK

NDL/R3997844

SOC/749325979

****

ARR/DET/CITE/CONV:

#1

04-10-YR-7 ARREST NCPD CC 211—ROBBERY

04-17-YR-7 PETITION SUSTAINED, JUVENILE COURT, WARDSHIP AND FORMAL SUPERVISION, TWENTY DAYS JUVENILE HALL

12-17-YR-6 VIOLATION OF PROBATION, PLACEMENT ORDER NINETY DAYS JUVENILE HALL

****

#2

12-03-YR-6 ARREST NCPD CC 459—BURGLARY OF RESIDENCE

12-17-YR-6 PETITION SUSTAINED, JUVENILE COURT, BURGLARY FIRST DEGREE, WARDSHIP AND FORMAL PROBATION, NINETY DAYS JUVENILE HALL CONCURRENT

****

#3

07-24-YR-4 ARREST APD IC 714—THEFT

07-24-YR-4 IC 714.2 CONVICTED, MISDEMEANOR THEFT FIFTH DEGREE: SEN. TWO YEARS INFORMAL PROBATION, RESTITUTION, FINE $400

****

#4

09-22-YR-1 ARREST NCPD CC 211—ARMED ROBBERY

ARREST AND CONVICTION RECORD OF VAL CAVARRETTA

RE: FOX, M. DCDA DATE: 10-08-YR-1 TIME: 1458
CIR/B2936567
NAM/01 CAVARRETTA, VAL
NDL/R3997024
SOC/749884535
PROBATION: EXP: 01-17-YR+2 CC 148.5—FALSE REPORT OF CRIME

****

ARR/DET/CITE/CONV:
#1
07-08-YR-10 ARREST NCPD CC 11357(b)—POSSESSION OF MARIJUANA, MISDEMEANOR
07-20-YR-10 PETITION SUSTAINED, JUVENILE COURT, WARDSHIP
09-09-YR-10 VIOLATION OF PROBATION, REVOKED, TEN DAYS JUVENILE HALL

****

#2
09-02-YR-10 ARREST NCPD CC 647(F)—PUBLIC INTOXICATION, MISDEMEANOR
09-09-YR-10 PETITION SUSTAINED, JUVENILE COURT, TEN DAYS JUVENILE HALL CONCURRENT

****

#3
11-10-YR-9 ARREST NCPD CC 11358—SALE OF MARIJUANA, FELONY
11-22-YR-9 PETITION SUSTAINED, JUVENILE COURT, FELONY SALE OF MARIJUANA, WARDSHIP AND FORMAL PROBATION, FORTY DAYS JUVENILE HALL

****

#4
04-03-YR-5 ARREST DCSO CC 11379—SALE OF METHAMPHETAMINE, FELONY
04-27-YR-5 CONVICTED, PLEA OF GUILTY, FELONY SALE OF METHAMPHETAMINE: SEN. 3 YEARS FORMAL PROBATION, 180 DAYS COUNTY JAIL

****

#5

12-10- YR-2 ARREST CC 148.5—FALSE REPORT OF CRIME, MISDEMEANOR

01-17-YR-1 CONVICTED, FALSE REPORT OF CRIME, MISDEMEANOR: SEN. THREE YEARS FORMAL PROBATION, SIXTY DAYS COUNTY JAIL

ARREST AND CONVICTION RECORD OF MARTY PAFKO

RE: FOX, M. DCDA DA DATE: 10-14-YR-1 TIME: 1505
CIR/A2211497
NAM/01 PAFKO, MARTY
NDL/D4925365
SOC/893136944

****

ARR/DET/CITE/CONV:

#1

05-03-YR-5 ARREST NCPD CC 496—RECEIVING STOLEN PROPERTY, FELONY

05-06-YR-5 RELEASED, INSUFFICIENT EVIDENCE (VICTIM REFUSED TO COOPERATE)

****

#2

07-13-YR-3 ARREST NCPD CC 500—RECEIVING MONEY FOR TRANSMITTAL TO FOREIGN COUNTRY, FELONY

09-16-YR-3 PLED GUILTY TO MISDEMEANOR RECEIVING MONEY FOR TRANSMITTAL TO FOREIGN COUNTRY, THREE YEARS PROBATION, $3,000 FINE

NOT TO BE DUPLICATED

ARREST AND CONVICTION RECORD OF PEPPER HACK

RE: FOX, M. DCDA DA DATE: 01-03-YR-0 TIME: 1505

CIR/B8688249

NAM/01 HACK, PEPPER

NDL/F7698847

SOC/550443678

****

ARR/DET/CITE/CONV:

#1

03-13-YR-6 ARREST NCPD CC 273.5—INFLICTION OF CORPORAL INJURY ON SPOUSE, FELONY

03-26-YR-6 PLED GUILTY CC 273.5—MISDEMEANOR, FORMAL PROBATION THREE YEARS, COUNSELING, NO CONTACT WITH VICTIM

11-14-YR-4 PROBATION VIOLATED, REINSTATED ON FORMAL PROBATION, NINETY DAYS COUNTY JAIL

****

#2

10-25-YR-4 ARREST DCSO CC 242—BATTERY, MISDEMEANOR

11-14-YR-4 CONVICTION, MISDEMEANOR BATTERY, NINETY DAYS COUNTY JAIL, CONCURRENT

****

#3

07-17-YR-3 ARREST DCS0 CC 148—RESISTING ARREST, MISDEMEANOR

09-29-YR-3 FOUND GUILTY IN JURY TRIAL, MISDEMEANOR CC 148. 120 DAYS COUNTY JAIL

****

#4

09-21-YR-1 ARREST NCPD CC 314.1—INDECENT EXPOSURE, MISDEMEANOR

09-22-YR-1 RELEASED, INSUFFICIENT EVIDENCE

Testimony at Preliminary Hearing

Testimony of Detective Alex Lowrey at Preliminary Hearing[1]

Direct Examination

1 My name is Alex Lowrey. I am a detective with the City of Nita Police Department. I have
2 been employed by the department for eleven years. I served in the Traffic Division for
3 my first two years, five years in Patrol, one year in Internal Affairs, and now three years
4 as a detective. During those years, I have worked a variety of cases, including homi-
5 cides, robberies, burglaries, other crimes of theft, and crimes against the person, such as
6 assaults, batteries, child molestation, and rapes.
7
8 On September 14 of last year, I was working the 1500 to 2300 shift, or 3:00 to 11:00 p.m.
9 I was at the station interviewing a witness to a stabbing murder when I got a call on my
10 police mobile radio to investigate an armed robbery that had just occurred at Miller's
11 Fine Jewelers at the Pavilions. I left immediately and arrived about seven minutes later.
12 Officer Rickert was already at the scene, and I took over handling the case.
13
14 Lexi Waitkus, the assistant manager of Miller's, was there and was very upset and
15 scared. Waitkus related to me the details of the armed robbery. Waitkus was extreme-
16 ly apprehensive that the suspect would return and carry out threats he had made to
17 Waitkus. I calmed Waitkus down enough to get a general description of the suspect,
18 which I radioed to dispatch for broadcast to police units. I did not pursue more details
19 as Waitkus was trembling and fearful of the robber's return and not in any condition to
20 be further questioned.
21
22 I examined the store carefully, noting the open safe that had a few coins, checks, and
23 bills in the bottom. I asked Waitkus to show me what objects the suspect might have

---

1 The transcript of Detective Alex Lowrey's testimony was excerpted so that only Detective Lowrey's answers are reprinted here. Assume that this is a true and accurate rendering of Detective Lowrey's answers. The testimony was given at the preliminary hearing on October 20, YR-1, in the Darrow County Municipal Court, Nita City, Nita.

1 touched so that we could check for prints. Waitkus pointed out the glass counter and
2 said the suspect had both hands on the men's watches counter at one time. Waitkus
3 also said the suspect reached in the safe to grab rolls of coins and currency. Waitkus
4 said because they had an unusual amount of currency on hand, they had placed it in
5 the safe, feeling that was a secure area. They have never had an armed robbery before,
6 just an occasional theft of an item. The robber seemed to be interested primarily in
7 the currency, as if he knew the money would be there. Waitkus said that the suspect
8 would had to have grabbed the brass handle on the inside of the door to get out, as
9 the door automatically closes when not in use, and it was closed after the suspect en-
10 tered. Waitkus said there were five silver dollars in the safe, which were apparently
11 going to be used for some key chains a client wanted to give as gifts. The silver dollars
12 were not at the bottom of the safe. I called for our ID Unit to send an ID technician,
13 and Supervising ID Tech. Jan Nicholson arrived and took interior photos and dusted
14 for prints.
15
16 After Lexi Waitkus had calmed down, I took a full statement getting all the details. Waitkus
17 was sure about being able to make a positive identification if Waitkus ever saw the rob-
18 ber again but repeated concern that Waitkus and other store personnel get protection.
19 I assured Waitkus that the department would vigorously pursue the case and would alert
20 Pavilions security about the problem. I told Waitkus that our department had an excellent
21 record of capturing armed robbers and that I had every expectation we would be able to
22 do so in this case. This seemed to comfort Waitkus.
23
24 After Nicholson completed checking for prints, we headed southeast down the Plaza to
25 take a photo and look for any additional evidence. I found a cloth bag lying in the gutter
26 about six stores down. I picked it up, and saw that it read "1,000 dimes." I looked inside
27 and saw a silver dollar lying in the bottom. I brought it back to Miller's, and Waitkus
28 immediately identified both as stolen from Miller's. I turned the bag and silver dollar over
29 to Supervising ID Tech. Nicholson.

1 I received confidential information that the defendant was responsible for this robbery.
2 On September 22, YR-1, I obtained a court order from Judge Landis to place the defendant
3 in a lineup. On that date, along with Officer Johnson, I contacted the defendant, brought
4 him to the station, and conducted a lineup. As expected, Waitkus was able to identify
5 the suspect and quickly picked out the defendant as the responsible party. I then took
6 a brief statement from the defendant, and pursuant to his consent, Officer Johnson and
7 I conducted a search of his apartment and car. I retrieved a baseball cap that appeared
8 similar to that described by Waitkus. Exhibit 6 for Identification shows the baseball cap
9 exactly as I found it. I then took a supplemental statement from Mr. Delaney. I compiled
10 the case investigation material in my report and submitted the case to the DA. The DA
11 agreed to file charges. I also checked out Delaney's claimed alibi and discovered that it
12 was unsubstantiated.
13
14 After Supervising ID Tech. Nicholson informed me that the defendant's print was on the
15 silver dollar, I also checked to see if there could be any explanation for his print, and by
16 checking with Miller's and Ben Bridge Jewelers, I determined that it was extremely unlikely
17 that the defendant could have placed his print on the silver dollar on any occasion other
18 than the robbery. That pretty well closed the case for us.
19
20 Exhibit 7 for Identification is an accurate depiction of the layout of Miller's as I remember it
21 on the evening of September 14 of last year. Exhibit 8 for Identification is an accurate map
22 of Pavilions Plaza as I saw it on September 14. Exhibit 9 for Identification is an accurate
23 map of Nita City showing the main arteries and the location of Miller's and the Plaza, the
24 defendant's residence, the jail and the police station, and Marty's Repairs.
25
26 **Cross-Examination**

27 The defendant was cooperative. He never refused to talk to me and permitted me to
28 search any area I wanted to. It is true that I would have needed a search warrant to search
29 his apartment and car, but he agreed to do this without talking to an attorney.

1 I did not check with any other people at Marty's Repairs to see if anyone remembered
2 the defendant being present there on the afternoon of September 14. I did not check the
3 names of employees working in other businesses in the immediate area of Miller's at
4 the time of the robbery, but I did make several inquiries to see if anyone had seen any-
5 thing and got negative responses. I described the suspect by appearance. I did not request
6 elimination prints be taken from Miller's employees and customers to see if any of the
7 recovered prints matched them. Yes, on direct examination, I did say that the fingerprint
8 on the dollar was that of your client, but I agree that the expert cannot say that is positive.
9 I really meant to say that there is nothing inconsistent with his print.
10
11 When I conducted the lineup, I did not hurry Waitkus in making an identification. As I re-
12 call it, Waitkus had no difficulty in recognizing the defendant but was simply being careful
13 before completing the form. I don't recall anyone else being in the immediate area where
14 Waitkus was located, but the lineup room is used for multiple lineups, and we could have
15 had a lineup either just before this one or another scheduled to go after. In that case, there
16 would be other people in the immediate vicinity. During the lineup, I did not have any of
17 the six men speak. The lineup was not photographed, videotaped, or recorded on DVD.
18
19 I did not record my initial interview with Waitkus or any of our subsequent discussions.
20 I don't know what you mean when you ask if I used a cognitive interview technique. I sim-
21 ply asked Waitkus to tell me what happened and then asked follow-up questions to get
22 clarification. I certainly did not suggest to Waitkus what the suspect looked like or who
23 should be identified. Yes, I am fully aware of the State of Nita's District Attorney's Asso-
24 ciation Lineup Procedure Guidelines. No, there was no other person in the room where
25 I was standing with Waitkus when Waitkus was looking at the lineup. Yes, all the men
26 in the lineup were wearing jail clothes. I suppose that would leave a witness with the
27 impression that there was an arrest. And, yes, the guidelines in Item 3 suggest the wit-
28 ness should not be informed that an arrest has been made and the police have a suspect
29 that the witness will be viewing. Yes, I am familiar with a "double blind" lineup; in that
30 procedure, the person conducting the lineup does not know which person in the lineup is

1 the suspect. Of course I knew which number the defendant had, number four. I suppose
2 I could have arranged to have a "blind administer" handle the lineup, but given the time
3 demands, it was important that the lineup be arranged and run as soon as we could com-
4 plete the process. And, no I did not use a recorder to record my comments and Waitkus's
5 comments. I did not have any of the six men in the lineup speak, so, no, Waitkus did not
6 have an opportunity to identify the voices of the six men. No, the men in the lineup did
7 not have an opportunity to pick the numbers they had. No, I did not ask if the defendant
8 would like his attorney to be present during the lineup.
9
10 I certainly am familiar with studies and reports of false eyewitness identifications, and
11 our department has taken considerable effort to comply with recommendations from
12 reliable experts in this field of study. I do not see any failures in this case to comply with
13 the State of Nita District Attorneys Lineup Procedure Guidelines. And, I certainly deny
14 that any outsiders other than men in the lineup had an opportunity to hear or see the
15 conduct of the men in the lineup or my conduct during the lineup.
16
17 I talked to Val Cavarretta about this case. The police made no agreement with Cavarretta
18 until the DA's Office approved it. We never gave Cavarretta any of the details in the case.
19 Cavarretta provided all the details to us in the interview. It is true that there was a story
20 covered by the *Press Clarion* that was on their website the next day on September 15.
21 There was one piece of information in the story that was incorrect, the part about quotes
22 from the suspect. Lexi Waitkus never told us the suspect said the word "withdrawal."
23 If Cavarretta had not made the agreement, our office would have submitted Cavarret-
24 ta's case to the DA and sought felony possession for sale of cocaine charges, a probation
25 violation, and state prison. I believe the state prison term would be lengthened because
26 of Cavarretta's prior sale of methamphetamine conviction.
27
28 I agree that Cavarretta is not a person whose credibility would stand alone without
29 some independent corroboration. However, as you were able to see in the police reports
30 you received before this hearing, there were portions of Facebook evidence that we also

1 considered as corroborating what Cavarretta's told us about the case. [Objection by de-
2 fense to references to Facebook evidence not offered in the preliminary examination,
3 and the Court sustained the objection and struck that portion of Detective Lowery's
4 testimony from the record.]

I hereby certify that the foregoing is a true and correct transcription of the testimony of Detective Alex Lowrey on October 20, YR-1, at the preliminary hearing in *State v. Delaney*, in the Darrow County District Court, Nita City, Nita.

Certified by:

Dana Sturgeon
DANA STURGEON
Court Reporter

Testimony of Lexi Waitkus at Preliminary Hearing[2]

Direct Examination

1 My name is Lexi Waitkus. I live at 955 North Erickson, Nita City. I am married and have
2 one child. I am the assistant manager of Miller's Fine Jewelers, which is located in the
3 Pavilions. I have held that position for about three years. Before that, I was with Ben
4 Bridge Jewelers in the Downtown Mall, where I worked for two years. I graduated from
5 Nita State College five years ago, with a degree in Marketing and a minor in Accounting.
6
7 Miller's handles a complete line of fine jewelry, generally in the expensive range. We employ
8 four employees including my position, the jeweler's position, and two clerks. In addition,
9 Mr. Miller, who is semi-retired, acts as the manager. For the most part, I run the day-to-day
10 operation of the business. The person who is next senior in line is Audie Passeau, who has
11 worked at Miller's for a number of years.
12
13 On September 14, YR-1, I was scheduled to be at the store from 9:30 a.m., which is one-
14 half hour before opening time, until 6:30 p.m., one-half hour after closing. The jeweler,
15 Mr. Williams, left at 4:00 p.m. that afternoon. The rest of the afternoon, only Audie Passeau
16 and I were there. Shortly before 5:30, Audie asked if it was OK to leave for a few minutes
17 and go to Nordstrom to pick up some recently purchased clothes. I said it was OK, and
18 Audie left. Maybe five minutes later, that's when the man came in. He was alone, he looked
19 in his mid-twenties, he was [**specify race per Required Stipulation #4**], and he wore a
20 light-colored jacket, a shirt that looked like some kind of team athletic shirt with stripes
21 across the center, and a baseball cap that I recognized was an Nita City Nighthawks cap.
22 I remember that because I had seen a game in the Nita Garden Center several years ago
23 and remember the Nighthawks. I started to make some comment about the Nighthawks
24 when he asked me what kind of stopwatches we had. I pointed to our counter where we
25 have a variety of watches for runners and tri-athletes. After maybe two minutes of looking,

2 The transcript of Lexi Waitkus's testimony was excerpted so that only Waitkus's answers are reprinted here. Assume that this is an accurate rendering of Waitkus's answers. The testimony was given at the preliminary hearing on October 20, YR-1, in the Darrow County Municipal Court, Nita City, Nita.

he asked me if we had additional watches that were multifunctional and were in a sport style. I said we had some in the back that were not on display, and I would bring a few out. I started to walk to the back room, and that's when it happened.

I first noticed him when I heard him say, "Quiet, now. Don't be stupid. Do what I say." I looked at him, and he had this gun pointed at my stomach. I was stunned. He then said something like, "If you don't want to be killed, do what I say." I think he said something about looking away from him, or something like that. He then said, "Get the money. All the money. Do you understand?" I nodded. He said, "Where is the money? Take me to where you keep the money." I then walked into the office area where we have the safe. I pointed to the safe and said, "It's locked." He said, "You had better know the combination, or you're out. Like three strikes out. Understand!" He then made a motion with his hand like an umpire would, with the thumb up, raising his hand from about waist high to above his head. I thought he meant he was going to kill me. I knew the combination and opened the safe quickly. I guess I was so scared my hand trembled when I was turning the tumblers. It took me a couple of times to get through it. I kept expecting to hear the gun go off. I have never been so scared in my life. Anyway, I got the safe opened, and he pushed me aside, reached in, and said, "All I want is the money, no jewelry." He then grabbed one of our coin bags that we had in the top of the safe and stuffed currency and coins in the bag. He did this with one hand while holding the gun in the other. We had a lot of currency in the safe because we had completed some cash transactions and had a stockpile of cash on hand for cash customers. We had intended to deposit most of it at the next bank run. As it turns out, when we checked our records, we had exactly $22,400 in currency, not counting a few rolled coins and five silver dollars. It looked to me like the man got all the currency, the silver dollars, and a few of the rolled coins, but he left some coins and all the checks.

The man then said to me, "Lie down. Lie down now. Don't get up for fifteen minutes or you're dead. Understand?" I said I did. He then said, "If you get up before then, I'll come back and kill you. I'll be watching you." I lay down, and I heard him leave. He left walking toward the front door. Maybe five minutes later, Audie came back in and found me lying down. I could hardly speak, I was so scared. Finally, I calmed down long enough to tell Audie what happened, and then I called 911.

I see the man in this courtroom who held me up. He's there at counsel table [the Court let the record reflect the witness identified the defendant, Ardell Delaney]. I'm positive. I won't forget his face as long as I live. I got a good look at him, and the lighting was very good inside the store. I have never had any question that I would recognize him if I saw him again. I don't believe that I have ever seen the defendant before September 14.

The detective, who came out to investigate the case, just before leaving showed me a bag containing a silver dollar. I recognized the bag because of the wording "1,000 dimes." In the bottom of the bag was a 1900 silver dollar. I checked our business records, and they showed that we had five silver dollars, one of which was a 1900. We noted these silver dollars, because sometimes customers want to use them in jewelry. They are particularly popular for key chains. Some male customers like to have them gold plated. The face of the dollar is called a "Morgan." The dollar in the bag was identical to one we had in the safe.

Cross-Examination

From the time I saw the gun until the detective came, I was so scared I could hardly think. I didn't want to do anything that would upset this man. When he said something about not looking at him, I knew I had better not look at him. However, I couldn't help seeing what he was doing when he reached in the safe. I was looking directly at his arm and the safe.

When the detective called me to tell me they had a suspect and asked me to come down for the lineup, I felt relieved. Obviously, I was very apprehensive that the person might later harm me, and I certainly wanted the person responsible for this terrible crime to be caught. The detective had told me earlier that they had a good record of catching armed robbers, so I felt they probably had the right man. I don't think I had ever seen any of the five or six men in the lineup before the date of the lineup. It's true that I subscribe to the *Press Clarion* and do read the sports page. I have followed baseball for many years and

1 have read about local high school and college games. The name Delaney sounds vaguely
2 familiar to me. I don't recall seeing his face in the paper before.
3
4 At the lineup, the detective told me that the person who committed the crime might or
5 might not be in the lineup. There were several people in the viewing room when I looked
6 at the men. I took my time. The detective did say something to me about how much
7 time I was taking, but I don't recall what was said. When I was through, I wrote what
8 I felt about the identification down on a form that I was given. If the detective told me to
9 hurry up, I think I would remember that, and I don't remember that happening, but I can't
10 be positive what the detective said.
11
12 I don't ever remember the man saying anything about a "withdrawal" before, during, or
13 after the robbery. If that had been said, I would have remembered that. I don't recall
14 which hand the gun was in. I think it was in the left, but it could have been in the right
15 hand. I know that it was a Nighthawks cap, and I'm sure I told the detective that when
16 I first talked to the detective. I am pretty sure I said something about the athletic shirt to
17 the detective, but I don't recall for sure.
18
19 Unfortunately, I can't track where we got the silver dollars. I don't have any records.
20 We have had them for some time, a few months to a year. I suppose it's possible that the
21 dollars could have previously been at Ben Bridge Jewelers, but I don't recall ever dealing
22 directly with them for silver dollars.

I hereby certify that the foregoing is a true and correct transcription of the testimony of Lexi Waitkus on October 20, YR-1, at the preliminary hearing in *State v. Delaney*, in the Darrow County District Court, Nita City, Nita.

Certified by:

Dana Sturgeon

DANA STURGEON
Court Reporter

Testimony of Val Cavarretta at Preliminary Hearing[3]

Direct Examination

1 I understand that if I testify today, I might incriminate myself. I have an attorney. I have
2 fully discussed the matter with my lawyer, and I am prepared to waive any rights and
3 testify. I have been told that anything I say today will not be used against me in my case by
4 the DA. I understand that if I testify falsely today, I can be prosecuted for perjury for any
5 false testimony, and I can be prosecuted for the charge of possession for sale of cocaine
6 for which I was arrested. That case is pending, but on hold while I cooperate with the DA.
7
8 I live here in Nita City. I don't want to say exactly where for security reasons. I have lived
9 here most of my life. I knew Ardell Delaney when we were in Poly High School. For a time,
10 we sort of hung out together during our junior and senior years. Ardell went on to the big
11 time. He was All-League and All-State in his senior year at Poly. He got a scholarship to
12 Nita U. and went on to become their best pitcher. Everybody knew Ardell was headed for
13 the pros and big bucks. When Ardell and I were at Poly, we used to share weed and some
14 pills on occasion. Nothing big. Other than seeing Ardell's picture in the paper, I pretty well
15 lost track of him after Poly until this past summer.
16
17 Sometime during the summer last year, I saw Ardell at a concert out at The Grove. I think
18 The Nasties were playing. I bumped into Ardell, and we talked a little bit about old times.
19 Then Ardell told me he wasn't playing ball because he had hurt his arm throwing too
20 much. I guess the trainer said he wasn't warming up right. Ardell said it would take sev-
21 eral months of healing and therapy to get it right, but he knew that he could play winter
22 ball for the Nighthawks farm system and hoped he would be in the majors next year.
23 He said he would like to find some good stuff. I wasn't sure what he meant and asked
24 him. He said, "Stuff." I said, "Weed?" He said, "No, good stuff. Coke." He told me he had

---

3 The transcript of Val Cavarretta's testimony was excerpted so that only Val Cavarretta's answers are reprinted here. Assume that this is a true and accurate rendering of Val Cavarretta's answers. The testimony was given at the preliminary hearing on October 20, YR-1, in the Darrow County Municipal Court, Nita City, Nita.

1 started using a little coke first at someplace called Gulfport, then somewhere in Iowa,
2 and then said he got some really good stuff in winter ball in the Caribbean. He said he
3 hadn't been back in town long, and didn't know where to get any. I told him I would let
4 him know what I could find out. I said, "How do I find you?" He said, "Easy, just call my
5 friend, Marty." He gave me Marty's number. I later called it and found out it was Marty's
6 Repair Shop.
7
8 I didn't want to deal any stuff. I had a little problem about five years ago where I fell on a
9 bum rap for sale of speed, and I didn't want any more problems with the law. But I knew
10 a guy called "Duke," a heavyweight, I've been told, in the business. I thought, "What the
11 heck, Ardell's an old friend." So I saw Duke at the adult store down the street and asked
12 him if he was interested in helping an old friend of mine. I told Duke who it was. Duke
13 had heard of Ardell. He said something like, "Oh, that would be good for business!" Duke
14 then told me he could deliver a half-key for sixteen grand but was only going to deliver
15 it to me, since he trusted me. To help out Ardell, I said that would be OK. I called Ardell
16 at Marty's and left a message. Ardell called me back, and I gave him the information, and
17 Ardell thanked me and said he would get back to me. He said he didn't have the money
18 right now, and it would take him a little time to put it together. I didn't hear anything for
19 a couple of months.
20
21 Sometime around a week before I got busted, I got a call from Ardell. He said, "Re-
22 member that little conversation we had at the concert about getting some stuff? Well,
23 I'm ready. I had to hit a jewelry store." He laughed about it. He knew he could trust
24 me. We had done time together in juvenile hall and, like I said, had hung out together
25 in school. I told him it would take me a couple of days to put the deal together, and
26 I told him I would call him when it was ready. He said I could still reach him through
27 Marty. Then on September 21 of last year I went to Duke's to get the coke, picked
28 it up, and Duke said I could pay him when Ardell paid me. I was driving back from
29 Duke's when the cop busted me and found the half-key. I never did get a chance to
30 call Ardell.

1 I am testifying today to the truth. The District Attorney has told me that the only way
2 I can get any support from them on my cocaine charge is if I tell the truth. That's what
3 I'm doing.
4
5 **Cross-Examination**

6 Before testifying today, I discussed with my lawyer the terms of an agreement between me
7 and the DA. As I understand the agreement, if I testify truthfully today, the DA would rec-
8 ommend to the court that I get what's called straight probation. That means no jail time.
9 I know that I am on misdemeanor probation right now, but I understand that won't be
10 violated. I understand that the DA won't file the prior sale of methamphetamine, because
11 if they did that, I would be ineligible for probation, and besides, that would add three
12 years to any prison term I got. The agreement is that I plead to the charge of possession
13 for sale of cocaine for probation. If I did not get that, I could do up to eight years in prison
14 plus get my misdemeanor probation violated.
15
16 I never said anything to Detective Lowrey about Ardell saying he "made a little withdrawal
17 from the jewelry store." I didn't use those words. Maybe the detective just misunderstood
18 me. I didn't see any story in the news about the robbery of Miller's. Sure, I check the *Press*
19 *Clarion* website from time to time, and that's when I saw Ardell's picture in the sports
20 section, and that's when I knew about his pro career, but I didn't see any story about the
21 robbery. I only knew about it when Ardell told me he had hit a jewelry store. I didn't know
22 any of the details except what Ardell told me.
23
24 Even though I said on direct that Duke was charging sixteen grand for the half-key, it was
25 fifteen grand, now that I think about it. I didn't see anything wrong, since I was the person
26 taking the risk, with Ardell giving me an extra grand. After all, Duke was giving it up on
27 my credit.
28
29 The police did ask me to take part in kind of a sting, where I was to call Ardell and be
30 wired up on a recorder. They wanted to get some kind of a recording of Ardell making

1 the deal. I wouldn't do it, because I wasn't going to be a snitch. I would tell them what
2 happened, but I wasn't going to go out and work the case like some snitch. No, it's not
3 true that I refused because I was afraid they would hear on the recording that he didn't
4 know anything about the deal. He knew what the deal was. He was the one that wanted
5 it. It was just because I couldn't do that to an old friend.
6
7 I certainly have corroboration about what I have said today. If you were to look at my
8 Facebook page and that of Ardell, you would see that I have told the truth. [Defense coun-
9 sel objected to this testimony as lacking any foundation. The court granted the objection
10 and struck this portion from the record.]

I hereby certify that the foregoing is a true and correct transcription of the testimony of Val Cavarretta on October 20, YR-1, at the preliminary hearing in *State v. Delaney*, in the Darrow County District Court, Nita City, Nita.

Certified by:

Dana Sturgeon
DANA STURGEON
Court Reporter

Testimony of Jan Nicholson at Preliminary Hearing[4]

Direct Examination

1 I am the Supervising Identification Technician of the Nita City Police Department. I have
2 headed that unit for three years. Prior to that time I was a Senior Identification Tech-
3 nician. I have been with the department's identification unit for the last eleven years.
4 My responsibilities are to supervise the ID unit's activities, including evidence gathering,
5 photographing, preparing diagrams, evidence analysis, and fingerprint lifting, compari-
6 son, and cataloging.
7
8 I have a bachelor's degree in Criminal Justice from Nita State College. I joined the Nita
9 City Police Department in YR-11 as an Identification Technician 1. My initial training
10 with the department was a basic course, Evidence Handling, put on by the State of Nita
11 Department of Justice that lasted one week. I then began on-the-job training from the
12 then Supervising ID Technician Mildred Merullo and Senior ID Technician Chris Kush.
13 Part of my duties consisted of going to crime scenes to look for and preserve fingerprint
14 evidence. In order to improve my skills in fingerprint lifting and comparisons, I attended
15 a three-day course, Fingerprint Pattern Recognition, put on by the Department of Justice.
16 Later in my first year of work with the department, I attended a one-week course on
17 processing and comparisons called Latent Print Techniques. In my second year of work,
18 I attended the FBI Advanced Latent Print Techniques one-week course. In my third year
19 of work, I attended a DOJ course called Specialized Latent Print Techniques. Through-
20 out the years, I have attended fingerprint seminars on a regular basis. The International
21 Association of Identification has about fifteen separate specialized programs, and over
22 the years, I have attended each. In recent years, I have given presentations on a variety of
23 topics, including a recent course on the use of super glue processing of prints.

4 The transcript of Jan Nicholson's testimony was excerpted so that only Jan Nicholson's answers are reprinted here. Assume that this is a true and accurate rendering of Jan Nicholson's answers. The testimony was given at the preliminary hearing on October 20, YR-1, in the Darrow County Municipal Court, Nita City, Nita.

1 I am certified as a Latent Print Examiner by the International Association of Identifica-
2 tion. This is the foremost such organization in the world. To receive certification, I need-
3 ed a bachelor's degree plus three years of basic experience—one of which must be in
4 classifying unknown prints—and two years of latent print examination. Applicants are
5 allowed to substitute two years of experience for each year required for a bachelor's
6 degree. Applicants are required to pass the certification test, which is a three-part test.
7 The first portion is a multiple choice examination, the second a five-card classification,
8 and the third is a practical test. The applicant must achieve a score of twelve out of fifteen
9 and cannot make any misidentifications. Generally, about 40 percent of the applicants
10 pass. We have two others on our department who hold this certification.
11
12 I have both lifted and made comparisons of literally thousands of prints in my career.
13 I have been called on to testify in court as an expert in the area of fingerprint comparisons
14 approximately 150 times. I am usually called by the prosecution, but I have testified as a
15 defense expert on at least ten occasions.
16
17 On September 14, YR-1, I was on duty at the Nita City Police Station and was informed
18 by dispatch sometime around 6:00 p.m. that a robbery had just occurred at Miller's Fine
19 Jewelers. We had only one ID technician on duty that evening, and because of the nature
20 of the call, I decided to handle the matter. I drove to Miller's and met Detective Lowrey,
21 who gave me details of the case. I took several photos of the interior of Miller's and then
22 began the process of dusting areas of the store that might retain fingerprints of the sus-
23 pect. Detective Lowrey and the victim, Waitkus, pointed out a glass counter above the
24 men's watches. I used a standard dusting process and was unable to develop any prints.
25 I was directed to a safe toward the rear of the store, and I used the same standard dusting
26 process. About two inches below the top inside the safe, I found and lifted latent prints,
27 which I labeled Latent # 1. I placed it in a department evidence envelope.
28
29 Detective Lowrey asked me to take an exterior photo. We moved east and then south
30 along Pavilions Plaza. Along the way, I took a scene photo. Detective Lowrey found a cloth

1 bag lying in the gutter. The detective seized it, and we took it back to the store. There,
2 Waitkus identified a silver dollar lying inside the bag as similar to that taken in the rob-
3 bery. Detective Lowrey then turned the bag and silver dollar over to me for evidence
4 handling and fingerprinting. The bag was not suitable for printing, but I felt the silver
5 dollar might retain prints. I placed the bag and silver dollar in a separate evidence bag.
6 I took both bags to the station. At the station I opened the cloth bag, removed the silver
7 dollar, dusted it for prints, and was able to find a latent, which I labeled Latent # 2. I then
8 placed both latents and the silver dollar in the evidence bags, which I placed in my locked
9 evidence locker.
10
11 On September 22, YR-1, Detective Lowrey called me and asked that I retrieve official fin-
12 gerprint cards of Ardell Patrick Delaney and attempt a comparison with the two lifted
13 latents. I did so. I was unable to match any of the prints on Latent # 1. However, in looking
14 at Latent # 2, I was able to find seven points of comparison with the left index finger of
15 Ardell Delaney. The seven points of comparison are displayed on Exhibit 5 for Identifica-
16 tion, which contains an accurate photo of Latent # 2 and of the left index finger of Ardell
17 Delaney. Points one and four are bifurcations, and the other five points are called ending
18 ridges. Seven points of comparison is generally not sufficient to make a positive identi-
19 fication, and it was not in this case. Most authorities in the field require eight, as I do;
20 however, there are some very experienced fingerprint expert examiners who will make a
21 positive identification in some cases on the basis of seven points of comparison. I can say,
22 however, that I noted no dissimilarities in the latent and the known print, and therefore
23 I certainly cannot rule out Mr. Delaney as a suspect.
24
25 I took a number of photos, which each accurately depicted the area or objects shown in the
26 photos. They are: Exhibit 1 for Identification of the interior of Miller's Jewelers, Exhibit 2
27 for Identification showing the condition of the safe, Exhibit 3 for Identification of the bag
28 containing the silver dollar as Detective Lowrey found it, Exhibit 4 for Identification of
29 the latent fingerprint removed from the silver dollar, and Exhibit 6 for Identification of a
30 baseball cap that Detective Lowrey said was taken from the defendant.

Cross-Examination

I took no elimination prints from any other subjects at the store, including Lexi Waitkus, Audie Passeau, Mr. Williams, Mr. Miller, Detective Lowrey, or any known customers of the store. Therefore, I have made no comparisons of the two latents with these individuals. I was not asked to compare any other suspects against these latents, including others who have been suspected of committing armed robberies.

Generally, coins are not good subjects for fingerprint lifting. The elevation of the surface of the coin creates problems. It is uncommon to get usable prints from coins, but it does happen from time to time. I can remember a nickel that was important in a case, which produced a very usable print leading to the capture of a suspect.

I cannot say with any degree of scientific certainty that the print on the 1900 silver dollar belongs to Ardell Delaney. If there were one more point of comparison, I would feel comfortable doing that, but with seven points I cannot say that. Most recognized authorities in the field agree with this standard and would not make a positive identification with seven points of comparison, but, as I testified earlier, some will. The average full-sized fingerprint of the left index finger would contain approximately 150 potential points of comparison if the print were in perfect condition.

Prints can be retained on a surface for many days, sometimes weeks, sometimes months, and even, on occasion, years. It all depends on the quality of the print, the nature of the surface, and the degree of protection of the print from moisture or contact. It is certainly possible that the print found on the silver dollar in this case could have been made by an individual on a date before September 14, YR-1. I cannot say with any scientific certainty that the print was not made back in the early part of YR-1. The position of the print is such that the finger was pointing straight up towards the top of the coin. The latent is positioned at the left edge of the coin, and it is consistent with the person holding the coin with the index finger on top and the thumb below. I am able to tell that by the pattern or configuration of the lines of comparison.

I hereby certify that the foregoing is a true and correct transcription of the testimony of Jan Nicholson on October 20, YR-1, at the preliminary hearing in *State v. Delaney*, in the Darrow County District Court, Nita City, Nita.

Certified by:

Dana Sturgeon
DANA STURGEON
Court Reporter

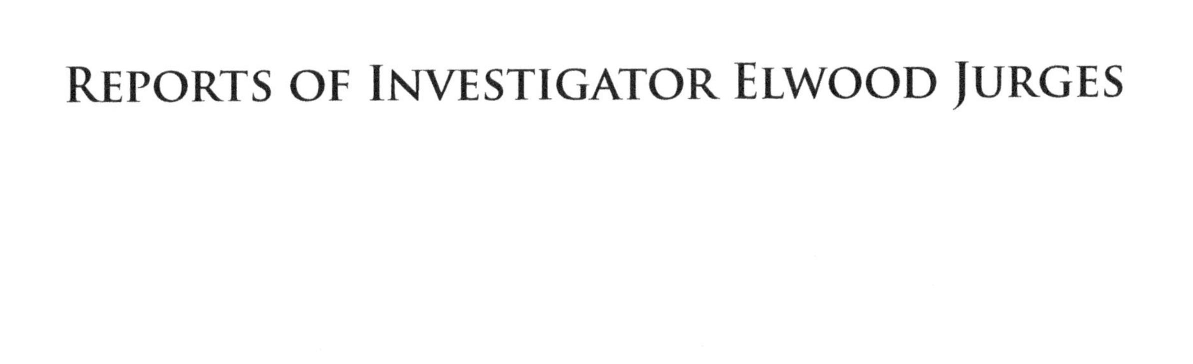

Reports of Investigator Elwood Jurges

Statement of Marty Pafko[5]

1 I live at 3914 Dallesandro Way in Nita City, directly behind my business, which is Marty's
2 Auto Repairs. I have known Ardell Delaney for many years. We were in school together at
3 Poly High. Ardell went his way, that is, he went to college and then to pro ball. I went my
4 way. I worked for a few auto repair shops and then opened my own business on Dallesan-
5 dro about five years ago. Once in a while I would see Ardell—usually when he came home
6 after playing ball, between seasons. Ardell knew that I worked on cars, and I generally
7 took care of his car problems. Back in the old days, Ardell's cars weren't so good, and they
8 needed work. Now he drives a nice Charger SRT.
9
10 I've seen Ardell several times since he got back from spring training. Apparently, he hurt
11 his shoulder, and the Nighthawks had to give him therapy and a training program to get
12 in shape for winter ball. We talked about it several times. I guess he was pretty faith-
13 ful about following the rehab program, because he was sure looking forward to winter
14 ball somewhere in the Dominican Republic, I think. Sometime around June or July, Ardell
15 asked if he could have people leave messages with me, as he was in and out of his apart-
16 ment. He didn't want to use an answering machine or a cell phone and said it was more
17 convenient. I didn't mind and told him it was fine, but he had better check with me in case
18 somebody really needed to talk to him. I would get a few messages, but not very many.
19 I vaguely remember getting a call from someone by the name of Val during the summer,
20 but I don't know the last name. When you ask if the name Cavarretta sounds familiar,
21 I couldn't tell you whether it was Cavarretta or not. That's the only call I ever remember
22 getting for Ardell from someone named Val.
23
24 Then sometime in early September, I got a call from Ardell. He said that he wanted to
25 bring his Charger over to have it checked for emissions equipment. He said something
26 about it not being approved by the Department of Motor Vehicles. I told him I would
27 be happy to look at it, but I was not an official emissions certification station, and he

5 This statement was given to defense investigator Elwood Jurges in his office on October 14, YR-1.

1 would have to get it finally approved at one of those stations. He said that was OK, and
2 on September 14 he brought the car over. It must have been sometime around 5:15 p.m.
3 I'm not exactly sure of the time, but I usually close at 5:30 and it wasn't very long before
4 closing time. I remember it was September 14 because the next day, September 15, I had
5 to get an order in for parts or miss getting the parts for another week, and I had not sent
6 the order in yet. I was still working on it when Ardell got there. When Ardell drove up,
7 I got up from my desk and walked outside. Ardell put the hood up, and I checked the
8 emissions equipment. I saw what appeared to be a damaged valve. I don't know how the
9 damage happened, but it could have been that it had been turned off, bypassing the emis-
10 sions equipment. I didn't want to work on it for a couple of reasons. First, I didn't have the
11 valve part. Second, if it was intentionally done to bypass the emissions equipment, then
12 that's against the law. I told Ardell he was going to have to take it to an authorized dealer
13 so they could correct it, and he said fine. I guess he was there maybe five to ten minutes.
14 I don't remember how he was dressed that day other than he was wearing casual pants
15 and a shirt. He might have had a cap on.
16
17 I don't have any records that would show the exact date or time, but I'm positive that it
18 was September 14. I told the detective that contacted me, but I guess the detective didn't
19 want to hear that.
20
21 I try and run an honest business. About five years ago, shortly after I started my shop,
22 the Nita Police Department accused me of using stolen auto parts in my repairs. I was
23 arrested. Three days later, the owner of the parts told the police there was a big mistake,
24 he knew me from our old neighborhood, and said I wouldn't do that, and said he wasn't
25 going to press charges. I was released.
26
27 Then three years ago, I was accused of taking money from illegal aliens who wanted to
28 send money back to their home country. All I was doing was helping a couple of people who
29 did spot work for me when they didn't know how to send money back to their relatives.
30 I just showed them how to wire money through a bank, and they paid me a small fee for my

honest + community

1 time. Some of the money apparently didn't get sent within ten days, which apparently the
2 law requires. I pled guilty to a misdemeanor just because my lawyer said if I was convicted
3 of a felony, I could lose my business license.

I have read the above statement consisting of two pages, and it is true and correct.

Signed: Marty Pafko   Date: October 14, YR-1
Marty Pafko

Witnessed: Elwood Jurges   Date: October 14, YR-1

Elwood Jurges

Statement of Pepper Hack[6]

I live in the town of Aberson in Darrow County about fifteen miles north of Nita City. I work as a weight trainer at Lade's Gym in Nita City. I don't know Ardell Delaney or anyone else in this case, for that matter. I'm offering this information because Mr. Jurges called me and asked me to come down to his office. Apparently, my lawyer and Delaney's lawyer were talking about lineups, and Delaney's lawyer found out that I had a lineup the same time as Delaney.

On September 21, YR-1, I was in Nita City working at Lade's. I took a break about three o'clock in the afternoon, and I walked over to a convenience store to get a few groceries. I walked through Borowy Park. Some child began pointing at me in front of several people. The child was about one hundred feet away from me. I had no idea what was happening, and I kept walking. I got to the market, got the groceries, and went back to Lade's parking lot. I put the groceries in the car and then went back into the gym. Around 5:30, the cops came in, talked to the manager, and then came over to me. They told me that they were placing me under arrest for suspicion of indecent exposure. I told them this was a mistake, that I had never done anything like that. It turns out this child in the park thought I was the one who apparently had done this in the park a few days before. The cop said that they were going to conduct a lineup. I sat in jail a whole day before they put the lineup together.

The next day, a little while before four o'clock in the afternoon, the cops came over to the jail and said they were ready for the lineup. They took me to the lineup room in the jail. We were sitting at the side of the room waiting for the last lineup to finish. I saw six men in the lineup, and the cops had this witness there. The witness was taking a long time, just looking. The detective in charge kept saying to the witness, "Come on, you saw this guy before. Let's finish this up." The witness said several times, "I don't want to rush. I want to be certain." The cop said something like, "You didn't think we were going to arrest the

6 This statement was given to defense investigator Elwood Jurges in his office on October 14, YR-1.

1 wrong guy, did you?" The witness said, "No." Finally the witness said something like, "OK,
2 I guess we have to finish this sometime." The witness then filled out a police form. The
3 detective walked off muttering something I couldn't hear. I could see the six men clearly,
4 and I recognized one of them as Ardell Delaney. I knew him from seeing his photo in the
5 paper several times.
6
7 After they finished that lineup, they put my lineup together, and the child apparently
8 couldn't make an identification, and I was released. I called my lawyer and told her what
9 happened, that I was released, and told her that I was lucky, because the cops try and
10 frame people for things they don't do. Then I told her about Delaney's lineup. She appar-
11 ently got in touch with Delaney's lawyer, and then I got a call from you.
12
13 I've had some run-ins with the police before, and I know you can't trust some of them. Back
14 about six years ago, my former spouse and I had a little spat. One thing led to another, and
15 I had to defend myself. I only landed one blow, but the cops arrested me and I was charged
16 with a felony. Obviously, that relationship was over, and I had no objection to agreeing to
17 a no-contact condition. I was offered a misdemeanor and pled guilty and got probation.
18
19 Then the sheriffs a couple of years later arrested me for battery when I was working at
20 Smith's Athletic Club in Aberson. A new customer was being really aggressive and made
21 a move as if to shove me. I pushed him down and he swore out a complaint. I made a
22 big mistake and went to trial before a judge, and I was found guilty, my probation was
23 violated, and I had to do three months in jail.
24
25 The last time I got stopped for what they called exhibition of speed. My foot just slipped
26 off the clutch causing my tires to squeal. I told the cop what happened, but she wrote me
27 up. I said I wasn't going to sign the ticket and the cop claimed that I tried to get back in
28 my car and take off, but that wasn't true. This time, my lawyer and I took it to jury trial.
29 I found out that the jurors are just as dumb as the judges. They believed the cop and found
30 me guilty, and so I had to do four months in jail.

1 I don't want to see someone else victimized like I have been by the cops of this town.
2 That's why I'm coming forward.

I have read the above statement consisting of two pages, and it is true and correct.

Signed: PEPPER HACK Date: October 14, YR-1
Pepper Hack

Witnessed: Elwood Jurges Date: October 14, YR-1
Elwood Jurges

Scheffing Psychological Consulting Services

995 Professional Drive, Suite 200
Nita City, Nita 55054
(121) 555-6684

November 7, YR-1

Landon Mack, Esq.
Hamner Mack & Schmitz
848 Stock Drive
Nita City, Nita 55058

Re: Your Client Ardell Patrick Delaney

Dear Mr. Mack:

Thank you for your referral of Mr. Delaney's case. As you requested, I have reviewed the case materials, which you submitted. Those materials are the transcripts of the testimony of witnesses Detective Lowrey, Lexi Waitkus, Val Cavarretta, and Jan Nicholson at the preliminary hearing; the police reports prepared by Detective Lowrey, Officer Johnson, and Jan Nicholson; the identification form signed by Lexi Waitkus; and the statements of Marty Pafko and Pepper Hack. I have also enclosed a copy of my curriculum vitae.

In this report, I will explain the common misconceptions about eyewitness testimony; the general process by which people, through the memory process, record, store, and retrieve information; and a number of factors in this case that could have led to difficulties in securing an accurate eyewitness identification.

COMMON MISCONCEPTIONS ABOUT EYEWITNESS IDENTIFICATION

People in general, and jurors in particular, commonly believe that an eyewitness account is strengthened by the witness's confidence and by the witness's ability to remember peripheral details. Research shows that neither contributes to the accuracy of the account.

Prosecutors argue, and jurors believe, that the more violent the event, the more likely that the witness is to be accurate. In fact, the element of violence tends to detract from the accuracy of the account.

Studies have shown that people are more likely to believe an eyewitness account than other forms of evidence, even when the eyewitness is incorrect. This is believed to be the result of the method by which the evidence is generally presented; that is, in a storytelling format, which is particularly effective in persuading people.

Therefore, it is imperative that these misconceptions about the reliability of eyewitness identification be dealt with effectively by the trial attorney. While attorneys may attempt to present treatise citations and other reference to authorities, commonly the only permissible—and effective—way to prove the unreliability of eyewitness testimony is through the presentation of expert testimony.

THE HUMAN MEMORY PROCESS

People record important events in a three-stage process. First, the witness perceives the event and stores it, in what is called the acquisition stage. This is followed by the retention stage, during which the witness has stored the memory but has not yet retrieved it. Finally, the witness attempts to recall the event. This is called the retrieval stage. A number of factors at each stage can affect the reliability of the eyewitness testimony.

Acquisition Stage

Event Factors

1. LIGHTING CONDITIONS. The amount of light available during an event can impact memory, whether it is too little light, as in a shadowed or nighttime incident, or too much, as in bright light glaring into the eyes of the witness. Here, according to both the detective and the victim, the lighting was good both at the scene and in the lineup room. There does not appear to be any apparent problem in lighting or in quickly adapting to lighting conditions. However, when examining the conditions under which the victim saw the suspect, the victim's statement indicated that the suspect's cap was pulled down over much of the upper portion of his face. This can create shadows that distort the features, affecting perception and identification.

2. DURATION OF EVENT. Witnesses are able to better identify facts viewed over a longer period. In reviewing the police report and the testimony of Lexi Waitkus, no time estimate was given concerning the duration of the event. However, Waitkus's statement and testimony establish that there was nothing unusual or important about the suspect's presence until he threatened the victim. The victim was then told not to look at the suspect, and presumably the victim complied. From that point, they walked to the safe, the victim opened the safe, and the suspect took the money and left. The passage of time would certainly be no more than a few minutes.

People tend to overestimate, rather than underestimate, the duration of an event. This has been established repeatedly by peer reviewed psychological studies.[a] Whatever time estimate the victim might give should be evaluated accordingly.

When these factors are considered in this case, it is reasonably possible that Waitkus never had a good view of the suspect after the importance of the suspect's identity became apparent. This becomes central not only in examining the reliability of the identification of the face of the suspect, but also the height, weight, hair color, and clothing of the suspect, including the type of cap worn. The correct inquiry here ought to be, how long did Waitkus focus on the face, body, and clothing of the suspect?

a. Laughery et al., *Recognition of Human Faces: Effects of Target Exposure Time, Target Position, Pose Position, and Type of Photograph*, 55 J. APPLIED PSYCHOL. 477 (1971); MARSHALL, LAW AND PSYCHOLOGY IN CONFLICT (Anchor Books 1969)(1966).

3. VIOLENCE. As I stated earlier, people have a general misconception about the effect of violence on a witness's ability to recognize and remember an event or make an identification. Studies show the accuracy of testimony in violent events is diminished.[b] Even memory of events and perceptions occurring prior to the violence is adversely affected by the subsequent violence.[c] It is true that people sometimes retain graphic memories of traumatic events, a phenomenon referred to as a "flashbulb memory." Such information may be retained vividly from a major traumatic event that would not be retained in ordinary events, but studies show that even in major events, the memory process over time can alter or significantly change details—the perfect picture that a person feels is "burned into their retinas" may in fact contain completely false specifics. People tend to remember the traumatic event but do not remember accurately details of the event. Reasons for this include the preoccupation with self, distraction, and narrowed focus and selectivity.

In this case, the threats of death and the presence of a gun produced perhaps the most traumatic event in the life of Lexi Waitkus. While Waitkus would certainly recall vividly the event itself, there is good, scientific reason to seriously question whether Waitkus would have sufficiently focused on details such as the face and clothing in a reflective way that would permit accurate recall.

Witness Factors

1. STRESS AND FEAR. The external factor of violence and the resultant internal stress are necessarily related. A traumatic event does not produce a "flashback" giving a credible recollection. The anxiety associated with heavy stress causes physiological and psychological reactions. In moments of heavy stress, the level of performance of an individual and the ability to remember details is severely and adversely affected. This results from people under such circumstances concentrating on just a few features of their environment and ignoring others.

Lexi Waitkus stated under oath at the preliminary hearing that, "I have never been so scared in my life," and that Waitkus's hand was trembling sufficiently that it took several times to dial the combination. Such actions and mental state are consistent with extreme stress. Such stress would adversely affect Waitkus's perception and concentration on details.

2. WEAPON FOCUS. Research shows that people tend to fixate visually on unusual objects.[d] Studies specifically dealing with weapons show individuals direct their focus to weapons and at the same time have a reduced ability to identify the suspect.[e]

In this case the weapon focus of Waitkus is set out at page 86 of the preliminary hearing transcript. When one considers that the suspect ordered Waitkus not to look at him, that Waitkus mainly looked at the safe and the arm of the suspect after that, and that the suspect's face was partially

---

b. Clifford & Hollin, *Effects of the Type of Incident and the Number of Perpetrators on Eyewitness Memory*, 66 J. APPLIED PSYCHOL. 364 (1981); Clifford & Scott, Individual and Situational Factors in Eyewitness Testimony, 63 J. APPLIED PSYCHOL. 352 (1978).

c. Loftus & Burns, *Mental Shock Can Produce Retrograde Amnesia*, 19 MEMORY & COGNITION 318 (1982).

d. Loftus & Mackworth, *Cognitive Determinants of Fixation Location During Picture Viewing*, 4 J. EXPERIMENTAL PSYCHOL.: HUMAN PERCEPTION & PERFORMANCE 565 (1978).

e. Loftus et al., *Some Facts About "Weapon Focus,"* 11 LAW & HUMAN BEHAV. 55-62 (1987); SHAW & SKOLNICK, SEX DIFFERENCES, WEAPON FOCUS AND EYEWITNESS RELIABILITY 413 (1984).

covered by the cap, it is likely that Waitkus failed to focus on the suspect's face during the traumatic portion of the event.

Retention Stage

1. STORING IN MEMORY. It is a fundamental fact that information cannot be stored if it was not perceived. The foregoing discussion deals with the perception or acquisition of information. After the information is acquired, many factors can influence the accuracy with which the information is stored. Those factors include forgetting or purging information or altering the information because of intervening events.

2. POST-EVENT MEMORY ALTERATION. Some experts feel that information acquired after the event can alter and distort the recorded information.[f] Others argue that subsequently acquired information merely suppresses the original information and makes it less accessible.[g] This often occurs when the witness discusses the event with others, such as other witnesses or police officers, or reads news accounts of the event. The new information can suggest facts that then become incorporated in the memory of the witness, with the witness then reporting that information as if it actually occurred. It is also true that details of violent events are more likely to be altered or suppressed by post-event misinformation, since the initial memory tends to be indistinct due to the stress factors discussed above.

In the present case, there are several post-event possibilities that point to the potential for altered memory. Waitkus initially gave little detailed information about the suspect. Eight days later, after Waitkus knew that the police had a suspect, Waitkus then made what could be described as a tentative identification of Mr. Delaney. Accounts differ whether the detective suggested the presence of the actual suspect in the lineup. The detective apparently gave a standard admonition that the suspect might or might not be present. However, if the witness Pepper Hack's account is to be believed, the detective appeared to be rushing Waitkus to conclude the identification, stating something like Waitkus didn't think they would arrest the wrong guy, and Waitkus responding, "No." All the circumstances Hack reported suggest that, despite the referenced admonition, the detective encouraged Waitkus to believe that the suspect was, in fact, in the lineup and should therefore confirm an identification. This implies that the follow-up investigation pointing to the identification of one of the six subjects as the culprit affected Waitkus's identification of Delaney. Waitkus admitted in the preliminary hearing to wanting the person responsible caught and feeling relieved (see discussion later under Circumstances of Lineup).

Waitkus obviously had the opportunity to discuss the case both with the detective and with the prosecution before testifying at the preliminary hearing. It is worth noting that then, thirty-six days after the event, Waitkus's memory had evolved from the uncertainty of "thinking" that the suspect is the lineup was the robber to a certain and positive identification of Mr. Delaney in the courtroom. The time period from the robbery to the preliminary hearing was exactly four times as long as the eight-day period to the initial identification. It is a fact that memory is self-reinforcing; people tend

---

f. Kohnken & Brockmann, *Unspecific Postevent Information, Attribution of Responsibility, and Eyewitness Performance*, 1 APPLIED COGNITIVE PSYCHOL. 197 (1987).

g. Bekerian & Bowers, *Eyewitness Testimony: Were We Misled?*, 9 J. EXPERIMENTAL PSYCHOL.: LEARNING, MEMORY AND COGNITION 139 (1983).

to remember things the way they want to remember them, in the most favorable light. It is a natural and subconscious process. If Waitkus perceived such an identification to be in Waitkus's self-interest, it is natural that it would grow stronger in time.

Retrieval Stage

1. EFFECT OF QUESTIONING ON RETRIEVAL. The manner in which witnesses are questioned can greatly affect the responses. Studies show that leading questions more often produce the desired answer, but not necessarily the accurate one. While leading is not allowed in court by the proponent, it is allowed and commonly used by investigators, lawyers, and others in preparing for litigation. The extent to which such suggestive questioning has occurred in this case can significantly affect the subsequent identification testimony by Waitkus. Unfortunately, the police in this case did not tape record the interview or discussions with Waitkus, and we will never know to what extent this unduly suggestive process was employed here. We do know, through Detective Lowrey's testimony at the preliminary hearing, that the detective was unaware of the issues that can be caused by this questioning technique and simply asked the witness to relate what happened and asked "follow-up questions." This is why many authorities recommend recording such interviews; the reliability of the interview and discussion process can later be tested, and jurors can be informed of any issue with the questioning techniques.

A technique for better assuring improved memory of Waitkus would have been to use the cognitive interview. That interview involves reinstating the context of the event, then asking the witness to report everything, then asking the witness to reverse the order of events, and lastly to change their perspective during the incident. To use this technique this instance, Detective Lowrey should have asked Waitkus to describe the details of the event from the beginning, then asked for a description of the events from the first moment of speaking to the robber. Detective Lowrey then should have asked Waitkus to describe the events from the moment of lying down on the floor and working backward, and then to imagine what it all looked like from the security camera's point of view. Studies have shown that the information given by witnesses questioned through this technique is significantly more accurate and complete than that produced by standard police interview techniques.[h]

2. CONFIDENCE FACTOR. As I stated earlier, the degree of confidence does not correlate with the accuracy of the information. The literature in the field indicates that eyewitness confidence is not a very good indicator of eyewitness accuracy.[i] This is especially true when the witness believes his or her recollections are important. By the time witnesses are called to testify at trial, they are often very confident, whether that confidence is warranted or not, and as the confidence rises, the witness's account strengthens.[j] When Waitkus now answers with a strong degree of certainty that Mr. Delaney is the suspect, that in no way gives any additional assurance of the accuracy of that identification. Such a change in the degree of certainty from the lineup to the court proceedings

h. Fisher et al., Field Test of the Cognitive Interview: Enhancing the Recollection of Actual Victims and Witnesses of Crime, 74 J. APPLIED PSYCHOL. 722-27 (1989).

i. Penrod & Cutler, Witness Confidence and Witness Accuracy: Assessing Their Forensic Relation, 1 PSYCH. PUB. POL. & L. 817 (1995); Wells & Murray, Eyewitness Confidence, in WELLS & LOFTUS, EYEWITNESS TESTIMONY: PSYCHOLOGICAL PERSPECTIVES (1984).

j. Cohen, "I Could Swear It Was Him, Officer," NEW SCIENTIST 11 (Jan. 18, 1997).

could well be evidence of the environment of the witness during the intervening time as opposed to the accuracy of the identification. This is supported by the fact that Waitkus could only initially say that the culprit was wearing a baseball cap with a red and yellow logo. Later, Waitkus was positive that the cap was a Nighthawk cap.

RECOGNITION OF PEOPLE

Now that I have addressed the general factors affecting human memory and their application to this case, I would like to point out specific issues dealing with facial identification.

Facial Features

The factors that most often are considered by people in making an identification are age, facial shape, and hair. Studies by authorities in the field have shown that if the subject identified is of the same age, has the same facial shape, and the same cut and kind of hair, there is likely to be an identification even if there are significant differences in other areas such as the eyes or mouth.[k] Therefore, if the subjects in the lineup differ in those prime areas, and one subject has the same general features, there is likely to be a mistaken identification. We only know that the subjects in the lineup were of the same general age, height and weight, and race, and that there were no unusual marks about the face. Without a photograph, we do not know the specifics about the facial shape or hair. It is possible that Mr. Delaney was the only subject in the lineup with the same general facial shape and hair as the true culprit.

Also, the lack of a photograph deprives any reviewer of the opportunity to determine by follow-up scientific study whether the lineup was unduly suggestive. This can be tested by showing such a photo to a group of individuals and giving them a brief description of the crime and the suspect. Statistically a fair and unsuggestive lineup would produce identifications of each subject one-sixth of the time. However, if the identifications were to show that Mr. Delaney was identified by these mock witnesses more than one-sixth of the time, the composition of the lineup would be unduly suggestive.

Lineup Procedures

As I mentioned earlier under Post-Event Memory Alteration, the manner in which the lineup was conducted is most important in any subsequent identification. The method of instructing Waitkus that the culprit may or may not be present was the correct, unbiased method. However, if verbal instructions suggested that the culprit was present in the lineup, then the lineup would be biased. Under such circumstances, there would be an increased risk of false identification by more than 100 percent over an unbiased lineup. Eyewitnesses are particularly likely to accept misleading information where the source is someone whom the witness believes is an expert, such as the investigating police officer.

k. Davies et al., *Wanted—Faces That Fit the Bill*, NEW SCIENTIST 26–29 (May 16, 1985).

Also, it is true that even in controlled studies with an unbiased instruction with the most favorable conditions, 33 percent of witnesses choose an innocent person in a lineup where the real culprit is not present.[l]

Subsequent Identification by Witness

In another study it was established that if the victim made an incorrect identification to begin with, such as at a lineup, that victim would do so again in court 78 percent of the time.[m] Here, the seminal event of making a tentative identification at the lineup assures by a three-to-one margin the likelihood that Waitkus, if originally wrong, would make the same identification again at preliminary hearing and at trial.

Unconscious Transference

This term is used to describe the phenomenon where the witness sees someone in one situation and confuses or recalls that person being seen in a second situation. There are a number of documented cases of such misidentification. It is impossible to say that such has occurred, only that it may have occurred. However, the factors giving rise to such an occurrence exist here, where Waitkus could have seen Mr. Delaney's photo previously, since Waitkus admits to following baseball. There is an additional possibility that Waitkus may have worked at Ben Bridge on a prior occasion when Mr. Delaney was present.

CONCLUSION

While it is impossible from my review of the case to say that any or all of these factors caused a misidentification in this case, I can say that there is a reasonable possibility some or all could have. This is why in such situations it is most helpful to have corroborative evidence such as video or audio recordings and photographs.

ADDITIONAL BACKGROUND INFORMATION

As I stated above, I have enclosed my CV. There are a few areas that need amplification. While my initial experience was academic, my later experience has been forensic. I made that transition in YR-7. Since concentrating on forensic psychology, I have qualified in court as an expert on forensic psychological issues on roughly forty-five occasions. I have offered expert testimony on the mental states of patients and clients in both criminal and civil cases. I have been appointed as an expert by judges in state and federal courts. I have qualified as an expert and testified concerning the memory process in repressed memory cases four times. Two of those were criminal, and I testified for the defense. In two civil cases, I testified for the plaintiff who was suing the therapist of a child. I have been retained as an expert in eyewitness testimony on at least twenty occasions and qualified as an expert and testified in court in nine of those cases, eight of which were for the defense and one for the prosecution.

---

l. Malpass & Devine, *Guided Memory in Eyewitness Identification*, 66 J. APPLIED PSYCHOL. 343–50 (1981).

m. Brigham & Cairns, The Effect of Mugshot Inspections on Eyewitness Identification Accuracy, 18 J. APPLIED SOC. PSYCHOL. 1394 (1988).

If I testify as an expert in this case, it is possible that the prosecution will seek to offer evidence of an opinion I gave four years ago in a federal criminal case. I was retained by the defense and testified that the questioning process employed in interviewing the victim of a rape case was unduly suggestive and therefore biased and could likely taint the later identification of the defendant. I further testified that the rape victim may well have been embellishing details because she was becoming more confident as the case progressed. Later, after the jury trial was concluded and the defendant was found guilty by the jury, the defendant gave a full confession to the probation officer and confessed that he had taken a video of the rape. That tape apparently confirmed the details testified to by the victim. If the prosecution seeks to develop this evidence and the court permits such an inquiry, I would like to point out that this in no way invalidates the research and findings of years of careful scientific study in this area. At no time during that case did I say that the victim was giving altered or incorrect information, but rather simply pointed out that the process could produce such results.

FEE STATEMENT

To date, I have devoted ten hours in case review, analysis, and the preparation of this report at the standard rate of $500 per hour for a total of $5,000. If you require my services as an expert witness in the trial, my fee will be an additional $2,000 plus any travel expenses. If you require additional information or would like to discuss the case further, please feel free to call me.

Sincerely,

Leslie Scheffing

Leslie Scheffing, PhD

Curriculum Vitae

Leslie Scheffing
995 Professional Drive, Suite 200
Nita City, Nita 55054

EDUCATIONAL BACKGROUND

BA, with distinction in Mathematics and Psychology, Stanford University, YR-16

MA, Psychology, Nita University, YR-15

PhD, Psychology, Nita University, YR-12

EMPLOYMENT HISTORY

Forensic Psychology practice, Scheffing Psychological Consulting Services,

YR-7 to present

TEACHING EXPERIENCE

Assistant and Associate Professor of Psychology, Nita University, YR-12 to YR-7

Adjunct Professor of Psychology, Nita University, YR-7 to present

Adjunct Professor of Psychology, Nita State College, YR-4

Guest lecturer, Stanford University, Darrow Community College, Glenback College, University of California, Irvine

FELLOWSHIPS

Fellow, Academy of Behavioral Sciences, Nita University, YR-10

MEMBERSHIPS IN PROFESSIONAL ASSOCIATIONS

American Psychological Society

American Academy of Forensic Psychology

American Psychological Association

CERTIFICATION AND HONORS

Certified, American Board of Forensic Psychology Examiners

Distinguished Contribution Award, American Psychological Foundation (Eyewitness Testimony), YR-9

Research Award, National Science Foundation (Human Memory), YR-8

PUBLICATIONS

Scheffing, L., *Comparative Reliability of Long Term v. Short Term Memory*, Journal of Behavioral Psychology (YR-13).

Miller, D.E. & Scheffing, L., *Examination of Computer v. Human Memory*, Journal of Computer Technology (YR-12).

Scheffing, L., The Effects of Age on Human Perception, Recordation, and Retrieval, Journal on Aging (YR-11).

Casparak, W. & Scheffing, L., *"That's Him. I'll Never Forget That Face,"* Constitutional Law Journal (YR-10).

Scheffing, L., *Recognition of Suspects in Violent v. Nonviolent Crimes*, Academy of Law Enforcement Journal (YR-8).

Donaldson, W. K., Moore, E.D., & Scheffing, L., *Dormant Memory Brought to Life*, Behavior and the Brain (YR-4).

Scheffing, L., Do Police and Prosecutors Corrupt Eyewitness Identification?, Nita Defense Counsel Journal (YR-2).

Scheffing, L. & Maxwell, R.W., *Let's Look Again at Repressed Memory Convictions*, American Association of Criminal Defense Counsel Quarterly (YR-1).

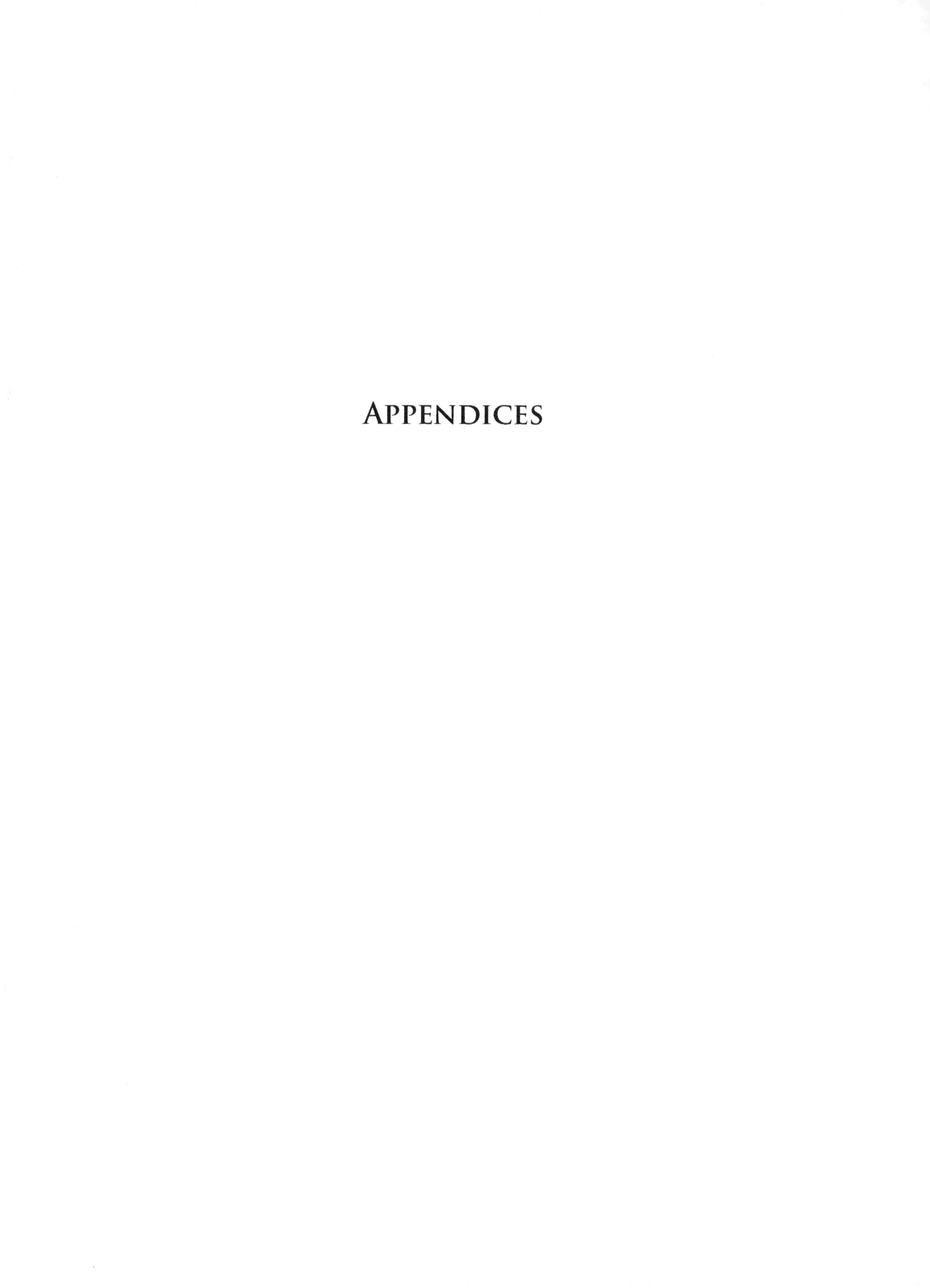

Appendices

Nita State District Attorney's Office

Nita State Lineup Procedure Guidelines
Nita State District Attorney's Association Best Practices Committee

1. Introduction:

There are various ways to conduct a fair and reliable identification procedure. The guidelines below outline how a neutral, fair, and reliable identification procedure can be conducted by the case investigator or by an administrator unfamiliar with the case. These guidelines are intended to allow for the individual needs of the thirty-two counties and 351 police departments in Nita State. The guidelines will improve with time as practical experience and knowledge is gained. Please check online to make certain that you are using the most recent version of the guidelines. The guidelines can be found at https://www.nsda.nita/best_practices/lineupproc.html

2. Definitions:

a. **Lineup**: A collection of individuals, either sitting or standing in a row, who are shown to a witness to determine if the witness can recognize a person involved with the crime.

b. **Suspect**: Person police believe to have committed the crime.

c. **Filler**: A person who is in the lineup, but is not a suspect in the crime.

d. **Lineup Members**: The people who make up the lineup; both the suspect and the fillers.

e. **Lineup Room**: Room where the fillers and suspect are arranged for viewing by the witness.

f. **Viewing Room**: Room from which the witness, the administrator, and on some occasions the defense attorney, view the lineup.

g. **Security Officer**: The person monitoring the fillers and the suspect in the lineup room.

h. **Administrator of the Lineup:** The person who is conducting the identification procedure. Depending on the jurisdiction and the circumstances of the case, a lineup administrator may be the investigator assigned to the case or a "blind" administrator. The procedures described in this document apply equally to both types of administrators. The types of administrators are:

i. **The Investigator Assigned to the Case**: The administrator of the lineup can be an investigator working on the case.

ii. **A "Blind" Administrator**: A "blind" administrator is someone who does not know which person in the lineup is the suspect. An identification procedure is considered "double" blind when it is run by a "blind" administrator.

iii. **Assistant District Attorney (ADA):** In some jurisdictions, an ADA and/or the investigator is in the viewing room with the witness and asks the witness If the ADA does not know who the suspect is in the lineup, then this is the same as a "double blind" identification procedure. The protocols outlined here apply equally to the ADA.

iv. **Supervisor:** In some jurisdictions, a supervisor participates in various stages of the identification procedure. The protocols outlined here apply equally to the supervisor.

3. How to Invite the Witness to Come In for a Lineup:

a. When an investigator calls a witness to arrange for the witness to view a lineup, the officer should simply ask the witness to come in for the identification procedure and should not say anything about the suspect. For example, the officer should say to the witness: "We'd like you to come in to view a lineup in connection with the crime you witnessed on (date and location)."

i. **Officer Should Remain Neutral:** The officer should give no opinions about the witness's ability to make an identification.

ii. **What to Avoid Saying:** Unless the witness specifically asks the investigator if someone is in custody, the witness should not be informed that an arrest has been made and that the police have a suspect that the witness will be viewing. For example, the detective should not say: "We have caught the guy, he had your credit card, and now we want you to identify him."

b. The administrator should instruct any officer or other employee asked to handle the witness to refrain from talking to the witness or victim about the case or the lineup.

4. Fillers for Lineup:

a. **Number of Fillers**: Where practicable, there should be five fillers, in addition to the suspect, but in no case should there be fewer than four fillers.

b. **Suspects**: There should be only one suspect per lineup.

c. **Similarities of Fillers**: The fillers should be similar in appearance to the suspect in the lineup. Similarities should include gender, clothing, facial hair, race, age, height, extraordinary physical features, or other distinctive characteristics.

d. **Identity**: Fillers should not be known to the witness.

e. **Fillers Seated**: All members of the lineup should be seated, if necessary, to eliminate any extreme variations in height.

f. **Suspect Picks Position**: The suspect should be allowed to pick his own position in the lineup. If there was an identification based on a photo array prior to the lineup, the suspect should not be placed in the same numerical position in the lineup as he appeared in the array (unless the suspect insists on that number).

g. **Requests from Defense Counsel**: Document any requests made by the defense counsel and whether they were granted, and if not, why not. Reasonable requests from defense counsel should be honored and documented. Any defense request for a change in the lineup that is not, or cannot be, honored must also be documented, including an explanation for the denial.

h. **Defense Attorney Cannot Speak in Viewing Room**: The defense attorney must be instructed not to speak in the viewing room when the witness is present.

i. **If Asked, All Lineup Members Must Speak, Move or Change Clothing:** If any lineup member is asked to speak, move or change clothing, all members must do so. Everything the lineup members are asked to do should be documented. If a witness's request of the lineup members is not feasible and cannot be accommodated, the request should also be documented.

j. **Fillers Must Remain Neutral:** The fillers must be instructed not to speak with each other or make any unnecessary gestures, but should remain still, hold the placard and look forward, unless instructed otherwise by the security officer in the room with the fillers.

k. **Photo Array Fillers**: Fillers from a photo array previously viewed by the witness should not be used as fillers in the lineup.

5. Instructions to Witnesses:

a. **Written Instructions for the Witness:** Provide written instructions to the witness. Such instructions should be available in various languages. The witness can sign the instructions after reading them, or after having the administrator read the instructions to the witness. This creates a verifiable record that the witness received the instructions, in the event of any challenge of the conduct of the lineup.

b. **No Comment by the Administrator Until the Identification Procedure is Completed and Documented:** Until the information about the identification procedure is documented, the investigator should not comment about the procedure or the next steps in the case. Stray comments that could potentially focus a witness's attention to one lineup member over the others, such as: "Are you sure you got a good look at number 2?" or "Can you take another look at number 6?" should not be made before, during or after the procedure.

c. **Give Instructions *Before* the Identification Procedure:** All instructions, both verbal and written, should be given to the witness *before* the identification procedure begins and not while the witness is in the process of viewing the lineup. This will alleviate confusion and minimize claims that the investigator somehow, even inadvertently, provided cues to the witness. Witnesses should also be told to take whatever time they will need when they view the lineup.

i. **Setting the Context:** The investigator should tell the witness that as part of the ongoing investigation into a crime that occurred on (*date*) at (*location*) the witness is being asked to view a lineup to see if the witness recognizes anyone involved with that crime.

ii. **Instructions to the Witness to Avoid Any Influence by the Administrator:** These instructions let the witness know not to look to the administrator for assistance in either making a selection or ratifying an identification. They also address the possibility of a witness feeling any self-imposed or undue pressure to make an identification. The instructions are as follows:

1) The person who committed the crime may or may not be present.

2) Do not assume I know who the perpetrator is.

3) I want you to focus on the lineup and not to ask me or anyone else in the room for guidance during the procedure.

iii. **Lineup Members Speaking, Moving, or Changing Clothing:** Consideration should be given to telling the witness that the lineup members can be asked to speak, move or change clothing, if necessary. However, if one lineup member is asked to do so, then all the lineup members will be asked to do the same.

6. Questions Asked After an Opportunity to View the Lineup:

a. After viewing the lineup the witness will be asked:

i. Do you recognize anyone?

ii. If so, what is the number of the person that you recognize?

iii. From where do you recognize the person?

b. If the witness's answers are vague or unclear, the administrator will ask the witness what the witness meant by the answer.

7. Multiple Witnesses:

a. **Witnesses Cannot Speak to Other Witnesses About the Identification Procedures**: If there are multiple witnesses who will be viewing a lineup, they should be told not to speak to each other about the identification procedure before, during and after the process. There are a number of ways to make sure the witnesses do not speak with each other about the identification.

The following are some suggestions that will diminish the opportunities that the witnesses have of talking to each other before or immediately after the identification procedure.

i. They can be kept in separate rooms before and after the identification, or

ii. An officer can sit with the witnesses to ensure they do not speak about the process or the case, or

iii. The witnesses can be allowed to leave immediately after participating in the procedure, or

iv. The witnesses can be taken to separate areas after the identification procedure for further interviews with investigators.

b. **One Viewing of the Photo Array**: In those jurisdictions that regularly use lineup procedures, consideration should be given to running lineups after the first witness makes an identification from a photo array. Where practicable, the additional witnesses can view only the lineup and not the photo array.

8. Procedures for Viewing a Lineup:

a. **Security**: Safety and security for all civilians, suspects, and law enforcement personnel must be ensured during any lineup procedure. Where necessary, the confidentiality of the witness's identity must be protected.

b. **Remain Neutral:** To protect the integrity of the identification procedure, the administrator must remain neutral throughout the procedure so as not to, even inadvertently, suggest a particular lineup member to the witness. Avoid comments that could potentially focus a witness's attention to one lineup member over the others, such as: "Are you sure you got a good look at number 2?" or "Can you take another look at number 6?" before, during or after the procedure. If a witness seeks guidance about whom to pick, the administrator should refocus the witness on the lineup.

c. **Administrator Standing Away from the Witness**: The administrator of the lineup should stand away from the witness during the lineup, in a neutral manner, while still being in a position to observe the witness. The key is for the administrator to stand outside the witness's line of sight while the witness is viewing the lineup. This will reduce any inclination by the witness to look at the administrator for guidance. When coupled with the type of instructions discussed above, this procedure will create a neutral environment, free of inadvertent cues from the administrator.

d. **Security Officer with the Suspect and the Fillers**: The security officer who is monitoring the suspect and fillers in the lineup room should remain out of view of the witness. This will eliminate the potential for any claims of inadvertent suggestions by the security officer and it also removes the potential for distracting the witness as the lineup is being viewed. However, if the witness needs a lineup member to speak, move, or change clothing, then the security officer in the room with the lineup members may have to be seen.

e. **Location of Lineup**:

i. **Neutral Location**: The witness should view the lineup in a room or area away from things that could influence the witness's identification, for example, other evidence in the case, wanted posters, sketches and other information about the suspect.

ii. **Central Location**: If identification procedures are conducted in a central location, away from the arrest precinct, a trained, neutral administrator, with no knowledge of the investigation may be available to conduct the identification procedure. A central location can be designed for a double blind identification procedure. However, the ability to construct and outfit a central location is a strain on resources and not available in the vast majority of jurisdictions.

9. Documenting the Lineup on the Lineup Form:

a. **Identification Procedure Protocols and Forms**: Develop standard instruction sheets, questions, protocols, and forms. Train all investigators involved in the identification procedure on the protocols.

b. **Photographing the Lineup:** Every time a witness views a lineup, preserve the lineup by photograph. The witness should sign the photograph, if one is available at that time, to verify that it is the lineup that he or she viewed.

c. **Documenting What the Suspect and Fillers Were Asked to Do:** Document anything the lineup members are asked to do (e.g., speak, move, or change clothing).

d. **Document All People Present for the Lineup:** Document all people in the viewing room with the witness and the lineup room with the suspect.

e. **Escorting Officers:** Document the officers who escort the witnesses to and from the lineup room, if any.

f. **Recording the Witness's Statement and Physical Reaction**: Write down, word for word, all comments made by the witness during the identification. The documentation should not merely state: "positive" or "negative" nor "hit" or "no hit" as the results. Record witness's words uttered during and after the identification procedure; for example, "It is definitely #1," "If I had to pick, it would be #2," "I'm not sure, but it might be #3," or "I didn't want to say inside the room but it was #4." The witness's words and physical reactions should be recorded.

g. **Follow-Up Questions:** If the witness is vague in his or her answer, such as "I think it is #3" or "It looks like #3," then the administrator should say: "You said [*I think it is #3*], what do you mean by that?" The witness's answer should be documented.

10. Speaking with the Witness After the Identification Procedure:

a. **Record the Witness's Statements First:** The administrator, or other appropriate person, should record the statements, comments or gestures of the witness regarding the identification procedure *before* talking with the witness about next steps.

b. **Discussing Next Steps:** Once the identification procedure is concluded and documented, the administrator can talk to the witness about how the case will proceed or what the next steps in the case may be, *e.g.* "We will continue to search for the perpetrator" (where there has been no identification), or "We will contact you about meeting with the assistant district attorney next week," etc.

After the identification procedure, witnesses frequently have questions about the case. It is entirely appropriate for the investigator to accurately answer questions about the case, including whether an arrest will be made.

c. **Do Not Comment on the Identification:** The administrator should not comment or make gestures on the identification itself by saying things such as: "Great job," or "We knew you would recognize him," or even nodding his head in agreement. Such comments or reactions may subsequently affect the witness's confidence in his or her identification. The administrator should remain neutral about the identification when speaking with the witness.

d. **Do Not Discuss the Identification with other Witnesses**: The witness should be told not to discuss what was said, seen or done during the identification.

State of Nita
Criminal Code and
Vehicle Code Sections

Section 148 N.C.C. Resisting Arrest

1) Every person who willfully resists, delays, or obstructs any peace officer in the discharge or attempt to discharge his or her duty is guilty of a misdemeanor.
2) A violation of this section is punishable by confinement in the county jail for up to one year, or by a fine of up to three thousand dollars ($3,000), or by both.

Section 148.5 N.C.C. False Report of Crime

1) Every person who reports to any peace officer, district attorney, or grand jury that a felony or misdemeanor has been committed, knowing the report to be false, is guilty of a misdemeanor.
2) Making a false report of a crime is punishable by confinement in the county jail for up to six months, or by a fine of up to three thousand dollars ($3,000), or by both.

Section 211 N.C.C. Robbery

1) Robbery is the felonious taking of personal property in the possession of another, from his person or immediate presence, and against his will, accomplished by means of force or fear.
2) The fear mentioned in Section 211 may be either:
    a) The fear of an unlawful injury to the person or property of the person robbed, or of any relative of his or her or member of his or her family; or
    b) The fear of an immediate and unlawful injury to the person or property of anyone in the company of the person robbed at the time of the robbery.
3) Robbery is either of the first degree or the second degree. Every robbery of any person with the use of a deadly or dangerous weapon and every robbery perpetrated in an inhabited dwelling is of the first degree. Every other robbery is of the second degree.
4) Robbery is punishable as follows:
    a) Robbery of the first degree is punishable by confinement in prison for six to twelve years.
    b) Robbery of the second degree is punishable by confinement in prison for two to six years.

Section 242 N.C.C. Battery

1) Every person who commits a battery is guilty of a misdemeanor.
2) A battery is any willful and unlawful use of force or violence upon the person of another.
3) A battery is punishable by confinement in the county jail for up to six months, or by a fine of up to three thousand dollars ($3,000), or by both.

Section 273.5 N.C.C. Infliction of Corporal Injury on Spouse or Cohabitant

1) Any person who willfully inflicts upon his or her spouse or other person with whom he or she is cohabiting is guilty of a felony.
2) A violation of this section is punishable by confinement in prison from two to four years or by confinement in the county jail for up to one year.

Section 459 N.C.C. Burglary

1) Every person who enters any house, store, or other building with the intent to commit theft or any felony is guilty of burglary.
2) "Inhabited" means currently being used for dwelling purposes, whether occupied or not.
3) Every burglary of an inhabited dwelling house, or inhabited portion of any other building is burglary of the first degree. All other kinds of burglary are of the second degree.
4) Burglary of the first degree is punishable by confinement in prison for two to six years. Burglary of the second degree is punishable by confinement in prison for one to three years or by confinement in the county jail for up to one year.

Section 496 N.C.C. Receiving Stolen Property

1) Every person who buys or receives any property that has been stolen or obtained in a manner constituting theft, knowing the property to be so stolen or obtained, is guilty of a felony.
2) A violation of this section is a felony punishable by confinement in prison for one to three years, or by confinement in the county jail for up to one year.

Section 500 N.C.C. Receiving Money for Transmittal to Foreign Countries

1) Any person who receives money for the purpose of transmitting the same or its equivalent to foreign countries and fails to either forward the money within 10 days, or fails to give instructions within 10 days committing equivalent funds to the designated person, or fails to refund the money within 10 days is guilty of a felony.
2) A violation of this section is a felony punishable by confinement in prison for one to three years, or by confinement in the county jail for up to one year.

Section 714 N.C.C. Theft

1) Any person commits theft when the person takes possession or control of the property of another, or property in the possession of another, with the intent to deprive the other thereof.
2) The theft of property not exceeding two hundred dollars ($200) in value is theft in the fifth degree. Theft in the fifth degree is a simple misdemeanor.

Section 10851 N.C.C. Auto Theft or Unauthorized Use of Vehicle

1) Every person who drives or takes a vehicle not his or her own, without the consent of the owner, and with intent either to permanently or temporarily deprive the owner thereof of title to or possession of the vehicle, is guilty of a violation of this section.
2) A violation of this section is a felony punishable by confinement in prison for two to four years or by confinement in the county jail for up to one year.

Section 11351 N.C.C. Possession for Sale of Cocaine

1) Every person who possesses for sale cocaine, whether natural or synthetic, or any salt, isomer, derivative, or preparation thereof, is guilty of a violation of this section.
2) Possession for sale of cocaine is a felony punishable by confinement in prison for three to five years.

Section 11379 N.C.C. Sale of Methamphetamine

1) Every person who sells, furnishes, administers, or gives away methamphetamine is guilty of a violation of this section.
2) Sale of methamphetamine is a felony punishable by confinement in prison for four to eight years.

Section 23152(a) N.C.C. Misdemeanor Driving Under the Influence of Alcohol or Drugs

1) Any person who drives any vehicle under the influence of any alcoholic beverage or drug is guilty of a misdemeanor.
2) Driving under the influence of alcohol or drugs is a misdemeanor punishable by confinement in the county jail for a period of not more than six months and by a fine of not less than eight hundred dollars ($800) nor more than two thousand five hundred dollars ($2,500).

Jury Instructions

State of Nita v. Ardell Patrick Delaney

PART I. PRELIMINARY INSTRUCTIONS GIVEN PRIOR TO EVIDENCE

01.01 INTRODUCTION

You have been selected as jurors and have taken an oath to well and truly try this case.

During the progress of the trial, there will be periods of time when the court recesses. During those periods of time, you must not talk to any of the parties, their lawyers, or any of the witnesses. If any attempt is made by anyone to talk to you concerning the matters here under consideration, you should immediately report that fact to the court.

Keep an open mind throughout the trial. Do not make up your mind about the verdict or any issue until after you have heard all the evidence, the arguments of counsel, the final instructions as to the law that will be given to you by the court, and until after you have discussed the case with the other jurors during deliberations

01.02 CONDUCT OF THE TRIAL

First, the attorneys will have an opportunity to make opening statements. These statements are not evidence and should be considered only as a preview of what the attorneys expect the evidence will be.

Following opening statements, witnesses will be called to testify. They will be placed under oath and questioned by the attorneys. Documents and other tangible exhibits may also be received as evidence. If an exhibit is given to you to examine, you should examine it carefully, individually, and without any comment.

It is counsel's right and duty to object when testimony or other evidence is being offered that he or she believes is not admissible. When the court sustains an objection to a question, the jurors must disregard the question and the answer if one has been given, and draw no inference from the question or answer or speculate as to what the witness would have said if permitted to answer. Jurors must also disregard evidence stricken from the record.

When the court sustains an objection to any evidence, the jurors must disregard that evidence. When the court overrules an objection to any evidence, the jurors must not give that evidence any more weight than if the objection had not been made.

When the evidence is completed, the attorneys will make final statements. These final statements are not evidence but are given to assist you in evaluating the evidence. The attorneys are also permitted to argue in an attempt to persuade you to a particular verdict. You may accept or reject those arguments as you see fit.

Finally, just before you retire to consider your verdict, I will give you further instructions on the law that applies to this case.

PART II. FINAL INSTRUCTIONS

02.01 RESPECTIVE DUTIES OF JUDGE AND JURY

Members of the jury, I will now instruct you on the law that applies to this case. I will give you a copy of the instructions to use in the jury room.

You must decide what the facts are. It is up to you, exclusively, to decide what happened, based only on the evidence that has been presented to you in this trial.

Do not let bias, sympathy, prejudice, or public opinion influence your decision. You must reach your verdict without any consideration of punishment.

You must follow the law as I explain it to you, even if you disagree with it. If you believe that the attorneys' comments on the law conflict with my instructions, you must follow my instructions.

Do not do any research on your own or as a group. Do not use a dictionary or other reference materials, investigate the facts or the law, or conduct any experiments.

REASONABLE DOUBT

The fact that a criminal charge has been filed against the defendant is not evidence that the charge is true. You must not be biased against the defendant just because he has been arrested, charged with a crime, or brought to trial. A defendant in a criminal case is presumed to be innocent. This presumption requires that the State prove the defendant guilty beyond a reasonable doubt.

Proof beyond a reasonable doubt is proof that leaves you with an abiding conviction that the charge is true. The evidence need not eliminate all possible doubt because everything in life is open to some possible or imaginary doubt. You must impartially compare and consider all the evidence that was received throughout the entire trial. Unless the evidence proves the defendant guilty beyond a reasonable doubt, he is entitled to an acquittal and you must find him not guilty.

02.03 EVIDENCE

You must decide what the facts are in this case. You must use only the evidence that was presented in this courtroom. "Evidence" is the sworn testimony of witnesses, the exhibits admitted into evidence, and anything else I told you to consider as evidence.

Nothing the attorneys say is evidence. In their opening statements and closing arguments, the attorneys discuss the case, but their remarks are not evidence. Their questions are not evidence. Only the witnesses' answers are evidence. The attorneys' questions are significant only if they helped you to understand the witnesses' answers. Do not assume that something is true just because one of the attorneys asked a question that suggested it was true.

As I explained to you at the beginning of the trial, if I sustained an objection, you must ignore the question. If the witness was not permitted to answer, do not guess what the answer might have been or why I ruled as I did. If I ordered testimony stricken from the record you must disregard it and must not consider that testimony for any purpose.

If, during the trial, both the State and the defense agreed or stipulated to certain facts, that means that they both accept those facts, and because there is no dispute about those facts, you must accept them as true.

02.04 DIRECT AND CIRCUMSTANTIAL EVIDENCE: DEFINED

Facts may be proved by direct or circumstantial evidence or by a combination of both. Direct evidence can prove a fact by itself. For example, if a witness testifies he saw it raining outside before he came into the courtroom, that testimony is direct evidence that it was raining.

Circumstantial evidence does not directly prove the fact to be decided but is evidence of another fact or group of facts from which you may conclude the truth of the fact in question. For example, if a witness testifies that he saw someone come inside the courtroom wearing a raincoat covered with drops of water, that testimony is circumstantial evidence because it may support a conclusion that it was raining outside.

Both direct and circumstantial evidence are acceptable types of evidence to prove or disprove the elements of the charge, including intent and mental state and acts necessary to a conviction. Neither is necessarily more reliable than the other. Neither is entitled to any greater weight than the other. You must decide whether a fact in issue has been proved based on all the evidence.

02.05 WITNESSES

You alone must judge the credibility or believability of the witnesses. In deciding whether testimony is true and accurate, use your common sense and experience. The testimony of each witness must be judged by the same standard. You must set aside any bias or prejudice you have, including any based on the witness's gender, race, religion, or national origin. You may believe all, part, or none of any witness's testimony. Consider the testimony of each witness and decide how much of it you believe.

In evaluating a witness's testimony, you may consider anything that reasonably tends to prove or disprove the truth or accuracy of that testimony. Among the factors that you may consider are:

- How well could the witness see, hear, or otherwise perceive the things about which the witness testified?
- How well was the witness able to remember and describe what happened?
- What was the witness's behavior while testifying?
- Did the witness understand the questions and answer them directly?
- Was the witness's testimony influenced by a factor such as bias or prejudice, a personal relationship with someone involved in the case, or a personal interest in how the case is decided?
- What was the witness's attitude about the case or about testifying?
- Did the witness make a statement in the past that was consistent or inconsistent with his or her testimony?

Do not automatically reject testimony just because of inconsistencies or conflicts. Consider whether the differences are important or not. People sometimes honestly forget things or make mistakes about what they remember. Also, two people may witness the same event yet see or hear it differently.

Neither side is required to call all witnesses who may have information about the case or to produce all physical evidence that might be relevant. The testimony of only one witness can prove any fact. Before you conclude that the testimony of one witness proves a fact, you should carefully review all the evidence.

If you conclude there is a conflict in the evidence, you must decide what evidence, if any, to believe. Do not simply count the number of witnesses who agree or disagree on a point and accept the testimony of the greater number of witnesses. What is important is whether the testimony of any other evidence convinces you, not just the number of witnesses who testify about a certain point.

02.06 EYEWITNESS IDENTIFICATION

You have heard eyewitness testimony identifying the defendant. As with any other witness, you must decide whether an eyewitness gave truthful and accurate testimony. In evaluating identification testimony, consider the following questions:

- Did the witness know or have contact with the defendant before the event?
- How well could the witness see the perpetrator?
- What were the circumstances affecting the witness's ability to observe, such as lighting, weather conditions, obstructions, distance, and duration of observation?
- How closely was the witness paying attention?
- Was the witness under stress when he or she made the observation?
- Did the witness give a description and how does that description compare to the defendant?
- How much time passed between the event and the time when the witness identified the defendant?
- Was the witness asked to pick the perpetrator out of a group?
- Did the witness ever fail to identify the defendant?
- Did the witness ever change his or her mind about the identification?
- How certain was the witness when he or she made an identification?
- Are the witness and the defendant of different races?
- Were there any other circumstances affecting the witness's ability to make an accurate identification?
- Was the witness able to identify the defendant in a photographic or physical lineup?

The State has the burden of proving beyond a reasonable doubt that it was the defendant who committed the crime. If the State has not met this burden, you must find that the defendant is not guilty.

02.07 WITNESS CREDIBILITY: CRIMINAL CONVICTION

If you find that a witness has committed a crime, you may consider that fact only in evaluating the credibility of the witness's testimony. The fact that a witness may have committed a crime does not necessarily destroy or impair a witness's credibility. It is up to you to decide the weight of that fact and whether that fact makes the witness less believable.

02.08 EXPERT WITNESS TESTIMONY

Witnesses were allowed to testify as experts and to give opinions. You must consider the opinions, but you are not required to accept them as true or correct. The meaning and importance of any opinion are for you to decide. In evaluating the believability of an expert witness, follow the instructions about the believability of witnesses generally. In addition, consider the expert's knowledge, skill, experience, training and education, the reasons the expert gave for any opinion, and the facts or information on which the expert relied in reaching that opinion. You must decide whether information on which the expert relied was true and accurate. You may disregard any opinion that you find unbelievable, unreasonable, or unsupported by the evidence.

02.09 DEFENDANT'S RIGHT NOT TO TESTIFY

A defendant has an absolute constitutional right not to testify. He may rely on the state of the evidence and argue that the State has failed to prove the charge beyond a reasonable doubt. Do not consider, for any reason at all, the fact that the defendant did not testify. Do not discuss that fact during your deliberations or let it influence your decision in any way.

02.10 EVIDENCE OF DEFENDANT'S STATEMENTS

You have heard evidence that the defendant made oral statements before the trial. You must decide whether or not the defendant made any such statements, in whole or in part. If you decide that the defendant made such statements, consider the statements, along with all the other evidence, in reaching your verdict. It is up to you to decide how much importance to give to such statements. You must consider with caution evidence of a defendant's oral statement unless it was written or otherwise recorded.

02.11 CORPUS DELICTI: INDEPENDENT EVIDENCE OF CRIME

The defendant may not be convicted of any crime based on his out-of-court statement alone. You may only rely on the defendant's out-of-court statements to convict him if you conclude that other evidence shows that the charged crime was committed. That other evidence may be slight and need only be enough to support a reasonable inference that a crime was committed. The identity of the person who committed the crime may be proved by the defendant's statements alone.

02.12 CONSCIOUSNESS OF GUILT: FALSE STATEMENTS

If the defendant made a false or misleading statement relating to the charged crime, knowing the statement was false or intending to mislead, that conduct may show he was aware of his guilt of the crime and you may consider it in determining his guilt. If you conclude that the defendant made the statement, it is up to you to decide its meaning and importance. However, evidence that the defendant made such a statement cannot prove guilt by itself.

02.13 MOTIVE

The State is not required to prove that the defendant had a motive to commit the crime charged. In reaching your verdict you may, however, consider whether the defendant had a motive. Having a motive may be a factor tending to show that the defendant is guilty. Not having a motive may be a factor tending to show the defendant is not guilty.

03.01 INTENT

The crime charged in this case requires a union, or joint operation, of act and wrongful intent. In order to be guilty of the crime of robbery, a person must not only intentionally commit the prohibited act, but must do so with a specific intent. The act and the intent required are explained in the instruction for the crime of robbery.

03.02 ROBBERY

The defendant is charged with robbery. To prove that the defendant is guilty of this crime, the State must prove that:

- The defendant took property that was not his own;
- The property was taken from another person's possession and immediate presence;
- The property was taken against that person's will;
- The defendant used force or fear to take the property or to prevent the person from resisting; and
- When the defendant used force or fear to take the property, he intended to deprive the owner of it permanently.

The defendant's intent to take the property must have been formed before or during the time he used force or fear. If the defendant did not form this required intent until after using the force or fear, then he did not commit robbery.

A person takes something when he gains possession of it and moves it some distance. The distance moved may be short. A property taken can be of any value, however slight.

A store or business employee may be robbed if property of the store or business is taken, even though he or she does not own the property and was not at that moment, in immediate physical control of the property. If the facts show that the employee was a representative of the owner of the property and the employee expressly or implicitly had authority over the property, then that employee may be robbed if property of the store or business is taken by force or fear.

Fear, as used here, means fear of injury to the person himself or herself.

Property is within a person's immediate presence if it is sufficiently within his or her physical control so that he or she could keep possession of it if not prevented by force or fear.

An act is done against a person's will if that person does not consent to the act. In order to consent, a person must act freely and voluntarily and know the nature of the act.

03.03 ROBBERY OF THE FIRST DEGREE: DEFINED

There are two degrees of robbery. Every robbery of any person with the use of a deadly or dangerous weapon and every robbery perpetrated in an inhabited dwelling is of the first degree. Every other robbery is of the second degree.

03.04 ALIBI

The State must prove that the defendant committed robbery. The defendant contends he did not commit this crime and that he was somewhere else when the crime was committed. The State must prove that the defendant was present and committed the crime with which he is charged. The defendant does not need to prove he was elsewhere at the time of the crime. If you have a reasonable doubt about whether the defendant was present when the crime was committed, you must find him not guilty.

04.01 CONCLUDING INSTRUCTION

When you go to the jury room, the first thing you should do is choose a foreperson. The foreperson should see to it that your discussions are carried on in an organized way and that everyone has a fair chance to be heard.

It is your duty to talk with one another and to deliberate in the jury room. You should try to agree on a verdict if you can. Each of you must decide the case for yourself, but only after you have discussed the evidence with the other jurors. Do not hesitate to change your mind if you become convinced that you are wrong. But do not change your mind just because other jurors disagree with you.

Keep an open mind and openly exchange your thoughts and ideas about this case. Stating your opinions too strongly at the beginning or immediately announcing how you plan to vote may interfere with an open discussion. Please treat one another courteously. Your role is to be an impartial judge of the facts, not to act as an advocate for one side or the other.

During the trial, several items were received into evidence as exhibits. You may examine whatever exhibits you think will help you in your deliberations. These exhibits will be sent into the jury room with you when you begin to deliberate.

Your verdict must be unanimous. This means that, to return a verdict, all of you must agree to it. You will be given a verdict form. As soon as all jurors have agreed on a verdict, the foreperson must date and sign the form and notify the bailiff.

IN THE DISTRICT COURT OF THE
STATE OF NITA
COUNTY OF DARROW

THE STATE OF NITA	)	
	)	Case No. CR 1909-YR-1
vs.	)	JURY VERDICT
	)	
ARDELL PATRICK DELANEY,	)	
Defendant.	)	
	)	

We, the jury, return the following verdict, and each of us concurs in this verdict:

[Choose the appropriate verdict]

______We, the Jury, find the Defendant, Ardell Delaney, NOT GUILTY of Robbery of the First Degree.

____________________ ____________________
Foreperson Date

______We, the Jury, find the Defendant, Ardell Delaney, GUILTY of Robbery of the First Degree.

____________________ ____________________
Foreperson Date